Virginia Women
1600–1945

Nay Madam h[appy] Virginias good
Genious Calls upon you and you designed to be a happy promoter of this
Heroyicke Interprize. . . . A woman to
have a Share of Honour in the Incom-
parable happiness to the Collony if not
as a Leader then as a cheife promoter of
the bussiness.

—*Virginia Ferrar to Lady Berkeley*
10 August 1650

Virginia Women
1600–1945

"A Share of Honour"

By Suzanne Lebsock

Virginia State Library • Richmond • 1987

Library of Congress Cataloging-in-Publication Data
Lebsock, Suzanne
Virginia Women, 1600–1945.

Rev. ed. of: A share of honour. c1984.
Bibliography: p.
Includes index.
  1. Women—Virginia—History. 2. Women—
Virginia—Social conditions. I. Lebsock,
Suzanne. Share of honour. II. Title.
HQ1438.V5L43 1986   305.4′074′0155451   86–23410
ISBN 0–88490–139–4

Contents

Foreword

Commissioned by the Virginia Women's Cultural History Project, this essay by project historian Suzanne Lebsock, of Rutgers University, originally appeared in the illustrated exhibition catalog, *"A Share of Honour": Virginia Women, 1600–1945* (Richmond, 1984). Founded in 1982, the project opened its major exhibition celebrating women's experiences in Virginia history at the Virginia Museum of Fine Arts in November 1984. Public interest in *"A Share Honour": Virginia Women, 1600–1945* was high, and the project sold more than seven thousand copies of the book during 1984 and 1985. The book also included a checklist and catalog by curator Kym S. Rice that documents the exhibition, and statements by Sue Ann Messmer, coordinator, Lynda Johnson Robb, chair, Helen Bradshaw Byrd, president, and Paul N. Perrot, director of the Virginia Museum of Fine Arts, that describe and commemorate the Virginia Women's Cultural History Project itself. When the Virginia Women's Cultural History Project ended in 1985, the Archives Branch of the Virginia State Library accepted the project's files (which are available to researchers) and the library accepted copyright for *"A Share of Honour": Virginia Women, 1600–1945*, which was out of print. As Anne Firor Scott, of Duke University, writes in the Introduction, this essay constitutes "a model for many other states" and a treasured addition "for libraries of professional as well as amateur historians interested in Virginia and . . . for high school students." This edition, published in response to many requests for copies, confirms Professor Scott's verdict that "rarely does one find so much sound research in so brief a compass in a form accessible to any literate person."

ELLA GAINES YATES
State Librarian

Illustrations

Captions for illustrations reproduced from *"A Share of Honour":
Virginia Women, 1600–1945* (Richmond, 1984) are based on those
prepared by Kym S. Rice, curator of the Virginia Women's Cultural
History Project.

Virginia Women
1600–1945

Introduction

By
Anne Firor Scott

Virginians have long been known for their deep interest in their own past—indeed, sometimes critics have complained that they live too much in the aura of past glories when they should be paying attention to a difficult and complex present. However that may be, it *is* a splendid past: Jamestown sustained, the first representative assembly in America created, the Declaration of Independence drafted, the Virginia Bill of Rights adopted, three consecutive presidents elected (while another Virginian presided over the United States Supreme Court), the University of Virginia founded on principles of academic freedom—not to mention all the glory, as well as the gore, of what well-raised southerners used to call the War Between the States.

All these events were the work of men and have to do with the public realms of war, law, diplomacy, and government. For many years the history books written about this state (and there were many) seldom mentioned a woman, except in the capacity of wife or daughter.

Since from fairly early on women were half the population, this fact is apt to strike one as a little odd. No less a personage than the late Douglas Southall Freeman remarked more than forty years ago that if Virginians really wanted to understand themselves and their values they should pay attention to the history of women. Few people were prepared to hear what he said, and historians went their accustomed way, writing about men and the things men do, and calling their work "history." There had been, to be sure, one major work dealing with the history of women in the colonial South published even before Freeman wrote, but, like his comment, Julia Spruill's *Women's Life and Work in the Southern Colonies* (Chapel Hill, 1938) was hardly noticed at the time and thereafter gathered dust on library shelves for thirty years.

Then in the 1960s things began to change.

There had always been some historians who went beyond or behind politics to the society itself, who examined the way people lived and what they thought about and what their most deeply held values were. In the 1960s this view and the kinds of questions it engendered began to spread. This new social history attracted many young scholars and gave rise to an ever-increasing amount of exciting work. The development in France and England of new research techniques, which made it possible to ask and answer questions about large numbers of hitherto unexamined groups, provided an added impetus to the growing concern with the history of society.

All this was going on as a resurgent feminism stirred many women to wonder about the lives and experiences of their mothers and grandmothers and all the other women who had lived and died unnoticed since the first European settlement. Some even began to wonder about the women who were here when the Europeans arrived and about the African women brought here against their will. Feminism also emboldened an increasing number of women to seek advanced training and to become professional historians. The combination of these developments has led to an explosion of studies about women and families that are remaking the historical landscape.

Women's history encompasses many things. Biography, demography, the law, work, homelife, public activity, voluntary associations, cultural values are only a few of the areas that have been examined. Historians of women have pioneered in the use of personal documents (diaries, letters, autobiographies, and memoirs) to reconstruct the way people have thought and felt in the past. Legal scholars have shown how much can be gleaned from court records, wills, and deeds. Archaeologists have taught us to look at material culture with a seeing eye. Women's work has been examined in economic terms. And so on and on.

Many of these findings have been published in scholarly journals, and so far comparatively few have dealt with the South. However, the quantity is growing and we know much more than we did even a decade ago. In years to come perhaps the Virginia Women's Cultural History Project will be cited along with other "firsts" of which the Old Dominion is proud, for it is a unique accomplishment. Thanks to the efforts of many people, a pathbreaking exhibit of women's material culture was created and shown across the state.

The monumental task of finding and then selecting documents, objects, and photographs was the work of Kym S. Rice, curator. This essay, designed to provide an intellectual framework for the exhibit, was the work of Suzanne Lebsock. It, too, was a major accomplishment. Lebsock searched scholarly journals and unpublished theses, books and primary sources, to explore the history of Virginia women. Together, Rice and Lebsock uncovered a wealth of material that illuminates the roles and experiences women have had in the Old Dominion. Rarely does one find so much sound research in so brief a compass in a form accessible to any literate person. One hopes this book will be a model for many other states. It will soon be a required item for libraries of professional as well as amateur historians interested in Virginia and will, I hope, be required reading for high school students.

A number of things become apparent to the reader of these pages. To begin with, one must be struck with how much more complex the social reality of the past becomes when one begins to ask what were the women doing? We see this in microcosm in Lebsock's description of the battle of Yorktown, hitherto always shown from a soldier's or possibly a politician's point of view. Suddenly we can see the war as a family affair, with all the ramifications that implies. Another way of saying the same thing is that history is perceived quite differently by people in different parts of the social structure. George Washington's history is not the same as that of Martha Washington—and certainly was quite different from that of the slave woman at Mount Vernon. The more we can see the stream of events from different locations the more closely will our view of the past approximate what really happened.

Not only do women experience life differently from the way men do, they also shape it differently. The record suggests that women care about some things that men do not value highly. Thus, the part women play in families and in child rearing perpetuates certain values. When women attain positions that enable them to affect political and social decisions, they often choose paths quite different from those approved by the dominant male ideology. We can see this happening in Virginia in the 1920s as the newly enfranchised women organized themselves to promote a legislative program focused on the needs of children—specific parts of which were opposed by some of their husbands. The long battle over child labor legislation illuminated the differences between the prevailing male values and those of women. In all the southern states the creation of state responsibility for public welfare was largely the work of women who used their own voluntary associations to create a political voice.

Reading these pages the thoughtful reader will begin to wonder whether the traditional periodization of American history needs revision if we look at the world through women's eyes. We have usually assumed that the important turning points have been political ("the early national period," "the age of Jackson"). For women the important turning points may have been such things as the identification of the cause of childbed fever, the availability of education, or the legalization of birth control.

Whether the reader agrees with these observations or not, he or she is guaranteed to find food for thought in this book. It is no mere bland summary of what women have said or done. Lebsock has not hesitated to offer interpretations of the way things were. That is as it should be; to provoke thoughts one must have thoughts.

But enough! The book itself awaits you.

1

"No Obey"

Women's Changing Status in the Seventeenth Century

In the early seventeenth century, people from three parts of the world converged in the land the English named Virginia. In 1600 all Virginians were Indians. Before long their claim to the land was challenged by the colonizing English, who needed laborers to work the land they took from the Indians, and who were willing to fill the bill by buying slaves, people forcibly imported from Africa.

In all three groups, of course, there were women. Reconstructing their lives is a delicate and at times frustrating enterprise, for the evidence is thin, and we are dependent on whatever the English—and English men at that—saw fit to write down. But it appears that not one of the three groups had what we think of as "traditional" sex roles. In Indian Virginia, for example, and in much of West Africa, women were the farmers. Among the English, meanwhile, ideas about the proper roles of women were often undermined by the fluid conditions of life and death in the New World.

By 1700 the English had established dominion over Virginia, and English men were establishing increasingly effective dominion over women. But none of this was a foregone conclusion in 1607. In the beginning, almost anything seemed possible.

•

7

From the writings of early English chroniclers, we learn of two powerful Indian women. One was Pocahontas, who, as legend had it, saved John Smith's head in 1607. The other was the queen of the Appamatuck, who had received an English exploring party a few months earlier. "She is a fatt lustie manly woman," wrote one of the admiring explorers. The queen wore a crown and jewelry of copper; she presented a "stayed Countenance"; "she would permitt none to stand or sitt neere her."[1] In other words, she reinforced her authority as rulers often did and in ways that Englishmen readily understood—by regal dress, by a dignified bearing, and by keeping her distance.

In the Indians' own language, this formidable woman was a *werowance,* the highest authority in her tribe. Among Virginia Indians, for women to hold such positions was not unusual, and the English, fresh from the reign of Elizabeth I (1558–1603), knew a queen when they saw one. What was more difficult for them to grasp was the importance of Indian women in the texture of everyday life.

At that time more than twenty thousand Indians lived in what came to be called Virginia. There were more than forty different tribes, and, while each had its particular territory and tradition, the tribes were clustered in three language groups. South of the James River were the Iroquoian-speaking tribes, the Nottoway and Meherrin. In the piedmont lived a number of Siouan speakers. About these groups we unfortunately know little. Most numerous and by far the best known were the Algonquian-speaking tribes of the tidewater region, among them the Appamatuck, Chickahominy, Mattaponi, Nansemond, Pamunkey, and Rappahannock. Long sharing a common language, many of these tribes had recently become political allies as well. Powhatan, the werowance of the Pamunkey, had inherited control of six tribes, and by the early seventeenth century he had wrestled two dozen other Algonquian tribes into a confederacy—some would say kingdom. The English, for their part, were impressed with the "terrible and tyrannous" Powhatan, just as he intended them to be.[2]

So centralized a political structure could not have been built without a sound economy, and the economy was based on the work of women. Women were the farmers in a society in which farming was the central occupation. "Their victuall," as John Smith put it, "is their chiefest riches."[3] Corn was the single most important product in the Virginia economy. During the growing season, the Indians drew together in towns of from ten to one hundred houses. Between the houses and sometimes on the town's edge were the fields, where women planted corn and beans together in the same hills (this way the cornstalks doubled as beanpoles and the land stayed fertile longer). They also grew peas, sunflowers, and several kinds of squash.

The Virginia soil was generous with wild fruits, berries, acorns, hickory nuts, and walnuts, and the gathering of these foods fell to the women. So did all of the food processing and preparation. The making of clothing was women's work, too. This meant, among other things, dressing skins and making thread "very even and readily" by rolling bark, grass, or the sinews of animals between hand and thigh; the thread was good for fishing nets as well as for sewing. Pots were usually made by women. So were baskets; and the weaving of mats was a major industry, for these were used both as furniture and as siding for houses. The women also had to carry the wood, keep the fire alive, and "beare all kindes of burthens," including their babies, on their backs.[4]

As for housework, there was little to do, for Indian houses were very simple—one room, furnished mainly with mats and skins. Made of bark or mats stretched over bent poles, the houses were snug and smoky, as fires burned along the center axis of the floor and the smoke was allowed to find its way out through a hole in the ceiling. It is not clear who built the houses in the summer villages. In winter, however, when the villagers separated into smaller groups and hiked to their hunting grounds, the women were once again in charge:

In that time when they goe a Huntinge the weomen goes to a place apoynted before, to build houses for ther husbands to lie in att night carienge matts with them to couer ther houses with all,

and as the men goes further a huntinge the woemen goes before
to make houses, always carrienge ther mattes with them.[5]

And what did the men do? One observer summed it up in a
single sentence: "The men fish, hunt, fowle, goe to the warrs,
make the weeres [fishtraps], botes, and such like manly exercises
and all laboures abroad."[6] The men, in short, hunted, fished,
fought, and made the implements they needed for each activity.
They also cleared the grounds for fields, though since they used
the slash-and-burn method this was not especially laborious;
they cleared away small trees and underbrush by burning, while
larger trees were stripped of their bark and allowed to die.

Since the English regarded hunting as sport and not as work,
they quickly concluded that Indian men were lazy, that the
women were drudges, and that the unequal division of labor
between the sexes was proof of the general inferiority of Indian
civilization. The English were wrong, for men did make sub-
stantial contributions to the Indian diet, even though the work
of women was more essential to the material welfare of their
people. English men and Indian men, meanwhile, had more in
common than the English knew, both "scorning to be seene in
any woman like exercise." The Indians and the English had
differing ideas about what was properly masculine and what was
feminine, but men of both groups assigned their own activities
more prestige than the activities of women.[7]

For all that, authority in Indian society did not belong to men
alone. Succession among Virginia Indians was matrilineal: Political power was inherited through the mother rather than the
father, and females were eligible to become rulers. John Smith
explained how it worked with Powhatan: "His kingdome des-
cendeth not to his sonnes nor children." Instead, Powhatan's
position would pass first to his brothers, then to his sisters,
"and after them to the heires male and female of the eldest sister;
but never to the heires of the males."[8]

Our knowledge of family life and family structure is otherwise confined to a few intriguing scraps of information; on the
whole, the English chroniclers were much sharper observers of

politics and the economy than they were of families. Sexual attitudes were somewhat different from those of the English, at least to the extent that women (whose individual status within the tribe is not clear) were sometimes offered as bedfellows for visiting male dignitaries. Some relatively wealthy men had more than one wife, and divorce was permissible. Parents were said to love their children "verie dearly." Mothers gave birth with no crying out, whereupon English men concluded that for Indian women childbirth was not painful.[9]

Would that we knew more. What we do know, however, adds up to an impressive record of female influence in Indian Virginia. And this is the significance of the Pocahontas story. Pocahontas was a girl with sparkle. Her name, according to the English, translated as Little Wanton; we might say playful, mischievous, frisky. She was about twelve in 1607 when John Smith made his first appearance in the immediate domain of her father, Powhatan. Uncertain of Smith's intentions, Powhatan's warriors killed two of Smith's men and took Smith himself prisoner. After three weeks of captivity and feasting, Smith was led to a large stone and made to lay down his head. The warriors raised their clubs as though "to beate oute his braines." Suddenly, Pocahontas sprang forth, the clubs were stayed, and John Smith was spared.[10]

Or so Smith told it. The authenticity of this story has been challenged many times, partly because in John Smith's earlier recountings of his exploits the Pocahontas episode does not appear at all, and partly because the dusky-princess-rescues-bold-adventurer theme was commonplace in European culture long before Smith set foot in Virginia. He could easily have borrowed it. On the other hand, it could have happened. In Indian warfare, women, children, and werowances were almost always spared. While male warriors were sometimes tortured and often killed, they, too, could be spared and adopted into the victorious tribe. Here the judges were women. Given women's importance as breadwinners and in the kinship structure, their deciding if and when a new person was needed made eminent sense. So Pocahontas could have saved John Smith after all.

What Smith experienced, although he did not know it, may have been a ritual of mock execution and adoption.

As time went on, of course, Pocahontas was the one who was adopted by the English. After John Smith's release, Pocahontas continued to live up to her name; she was spotted turning cartwheels through Jamestown, for instance. Her story took a more serious turn in 1613, when she was taken hostage by Samuel Argall, who hoped to use Pocahontas to gain bargaining power with the Indians. While living under English authority, Pocahontas met John Rolfe, who would one day achieve fame as the primary promoter of tobacco culture. They were married in 1614 and had one son. In 1616 they sailed for England, where Pocahontas was received as both a curiosity and a celebrity; early in 1617 she was presented to James I and Queen Anne. A few months later, just as she was preparing to return to Virginia, Pocahontas died. She was no more than twenty-two years old.

For a long time no one took much notice of her story. Then some one hundred and fifty years after her death, Pocahontas took hold of the American imagination as no other woman has. She was brought to life on stage, in verse, and in the pages of novels and of countless children's books. Her name was given to people, places, and an astonishing variety of things, from tobacco and quack medicines to cotton mills and coal mines. As powerful legends usually do, the Pocahontas story had several symbolic meanings.[11] But there is no doubt that the national romance with Pocahontas helped to soothe the troubled conscience of white America. Pocahontas had rescued one colonizer and had married another. She professed the Christian religion and was baptized Rebecca. She learned to speak the English language, sat for her portrait in English costume, and met her death on English soil. Symbolically, Pocahontas put an Indian stamp of approval on white people, white culture, and white conquest.

We could opt for a different symbol. The queen of the Appamatuck—the "fatt lustie manly woman" the English encountered in 1607—thought it all very interesting when the first explorers appeared. She looked the visitors over, fed them, and asked them to shoot their guns, "whereat she shewed not neere the like feare as Arahatec [the werowance of the Arrohateck tribe] though he be a goodly man."[12] The following year, when the English were desperate for food, she supplied them with corn. By 1611, however, she was alarmed. Launching an aggressive policy of expansion, the English began carving out plantations on her tribal territory. The queen of the Appamatuck decided to resist. She began by inviting fourteen colonists to a party. When the men arrived, they were ambushed and everyone was killed. Reprisal was immediate. An English detachment attacked her town, burned it, and killed everyone they could find, including women and children. The queen herself was shot, probably fatally, as she tried to escape.

Or we could take for our symbol the queen of the Paspahegh tribe. In 1610, the English governor engaged Powhatan in negotiations over the return of some Englishmen who had run off to join the Indians. Frustrated by Powhatan's "disdaynefull Answers," the governor ordered punitive raids on nearby tribes. The English marched on the Paspahegh's chief town, killed several people, torched the houses, cut down the corn, and took the queen prisoner along with her children. Returning to Jamestown by boat, some of the soldiers complained about the sparing of the children. This situation was resolved by throwing the children in the river and "shoteinge owtt their Braynes in the water."[13] On hearing further complaints about the sparing of the mother, the commander decided against burning and instead had her led away and stabbed to death.

This was unspeakable brutality, even for a brutal age. After Pocahontas married John Rolfe, an uneasy peace was established for a few years, but the basic pattern was already in place. Regardless of the Indians' strategy—be it aloofness, cooperation, or armed resistance—the determination of the English to take Indian land for soil-depleting tobacco crops was paramount. The brutality escalated. Under the leadership of Opechancanough, the Powhatan confederacy made a concerted effort to expel the English in 1622; this time women and children were not spared, and nearly three hundred fifty colonists were killed. The English reeled from the blow—and retaliated with extraordinary force. Somehow, after many years, Opechancanough's allies regrouped, and they struck again in 1644. By this time the English were far stronger, and their counterattack demolished the Powhatan confederacy. In a treaty of 1646 the surviving Indians were placed on reservations and promised protection in exchange for their help in fending off outlying tribes. Still, for the Indians there was no real safety. Whites were divided on Indian policy, and in 1676 the followers of renegade Nathaniel Bacon, Jr., made war on Indians of every description. A new treaty was signed in 1677, but in the meantime the Indians had suffered another bitter disaster.[14] Killed in battle, wasted by disease, driven out and starved out, the Indian population of Virginia by 1700 was perhaps one-tenth of what it had been a century before.

Among the survivors was Cockacoeske, the queen of the Pamunkey. In the treaty of 1677 all the subscribing tribes pledged their allegiance to her as well as to the English king. And as a probable reward for her loyalty during Bacon's Rebellion, the government presented her with gifts including a dazzling silver badge.[15] The English, it seems, were still willing to accept female political authority when they encountered it.

•

Virginia was named for a female ruler, of course, and the point was not lost on Virginia Ferrar. In 1650 Ferrar wrote to Lady Berkeley, the wife of Virginia's governor, offering encouraging words and a novel interpretation of history. Women, she claimed, deserved the credit for Europe's discovery of the New World. First there was Queen Isabella of Spain, who "to the Eternall honour of her Sexe . . . (though laughed at by all the wise Conceited Courtiers)" sent Christopher Columbus on his famous voyage of 1492. Then Elizabeth I of England ordered the "planting" of a colony in North America, "giving it as she was a Virgin Queene the Happy and Glorious name of Virginia." Next, Ferrar suggested, the governor's lady herself might continue the "Heroyicke Interprize" by funding an expedition to find a route to the East Indies.[16]

For Virginia Ferrar and many historians after her, heroism was found in exploration and conquest. For the women who helped colonize Virginia, there was heroism in survival. Wherever they came from—the British Isles, the West Indies, Africa—Virginia's new women faced a rugged existence. Thanks to Indian women, the colonists after a few years learned how to grow enough food to support themselves. Then in 1614 they began marketing the crop that would sustain their colony and run their lives. This was tobacco, of course, the seeds imported from the West Indies and the cultivation techniques once again borrowed from the Virginia Indians. Profits were high, at times spectacular, and so an entire society dedicated itself to putting more land in tobacco.

For the women life was not easy. The death rate was appalling. Living conditions were crude, and all but the wealthiest could expect a lifetime of hard labor. Yet, if a woman lived long enough, she could sometimes experience a surprising degree of personal freedom. If she began as a slave, she might become free. If she started as a servant, she might become a planter. If she were a member of a wealthy family, she might become a politician. In the rough-and-ready world of the seventeenth century, almost anything might happen.

The gentlemen of the General Assembly recognized women's importance. "In a newe plantation," they declared in 1619, "it is not knowen whether man or woman be the most necessary."[17] Believing that a permanent colony would not be established until the planters settled down and raised families, influential men had for some time tried to bring more women to Virginia. Decisions on who would come to America, however, were not made by legislators alone. Instead, they were made by hundreds of individuals, among them planters who decided that in the short run, on their particular plantations, men were the most necessary. The result was an extremely unbalanced sex ratio. Among blacks there were at least three men for every two

women. Among whites, men outnumbered women by three or
four to one.

The Virginia Company, chartered in 1606 to finance and
oversee colonization, resolved to send shiploads of "Maydens,"
young English women who would dare an ocean voyage and
marriage to a stranger on the other side. In her novel *To Have
and To Hold,* Mary Johnston later imagined the commotion
when the first group of maids arrived in Jamestown. "I saw
young men, panting, seize hand or arm and strive to pull toward
them some reluctant fair; others snatched kisses, or fell on their
knees and began speeches out of Euphues; others commenced
an inventory of their possessions—acres, tobacco, servants,
household plenishing. All was hubbub, protestation, frightened
cries, and hysterical laughter." The narrator drew closer and
heard some bargaining: "Says Phyllis, 'Any poultry?' "

> *Corydon:* A matter of twalve hens and twa cocks.
> *Phyllis:* A cow?
> *Corydon:* Twa.
> *Phyllis:* How much tobacco?
> *Corydon:* Three acres, hinny, though I dinna drink the weed
> mysel'. I'm a Stewart, woman, an' the King's puir cousin.
> *Phyllis:* What household plenishing?
> *Corydon:* Ane large bed, ane flock bed, ane trundle bed, ane
> chest, ane trunk, ane leather cairpet, sax cawfskin chairs an' twa-
> three rush, five pair o' sheets an' auchteen dowlas napkins, sax
> alchemy spunes—
> *Phyllis:* I'll take you.[18]

The legend of early Virginia was somehow brightened by the
tales of this strange marriage market, although the Virginia
Company in truth sent out only about one hundred forty
maids. Other English women made the crossing in ones and
twos, sailing with their husbands or following husbands who
had ventured over earlier. The vast majority of women colonists, however, were unfree laborers. Some, though their numbers were small in the first half of the seventeenth century, were
slaves brought by force from different parts of Africa (and from

Africa via the West Indies). About 80 percent of all English immigrants, meanwhile, were indentured servants. These people owed from four to seven years of faithful labor to whoever paid their passage from England. Until their time was up, they were not free to marry at all.

The new arrivals, single or married, bound or free, could expect rude beginnings. If, like the fictional Phyllis, her new household really contained five pairs of sheets, she would be doing very well indeed. The newcomer would need only a few seconds to size up her surroundings. From the outside the typical Virginia farmhouse looked (and was) small, and it probably needed patching. The inside could be inspected in three or four glances. This was a one-room house, measuring perhaps twenty-five by sixteen feet. It was a story and a half high and probably had a loft where children and servants slept. Otherwise one space had to suffice for every indoor purpose.

Except for its enormous fireplace, it was something like an Indian house, and like an Indian house it was sparsely furnished. Standard equipment for a house owned by a middling planter was one feather bed (not to say a bedstead), a chest for storage, a cooking pot, a mortar and pestle for pounding corn, an axe, some knives, a few wooden dishes, some odd spoons, and containers for storing crops. Stools and benches were not standard, although some households had them, nor were tables, forks, sheets, skillets, lamps, or candles.[19] Occasionally, some bright and beautiful object would light up a Virginia household, and some of the most prosperous planters lived in higher style. But the typical planter stuck to ruthless utility. If furnishings were spartan and houses leaked and leaned and all but tumbled down, no matter. The money was in tobacco, and the planter who wanted to succeed invested every spare shilling in laborers.

That, of course, is what brought most women to Virginia. Indentured servitude was the system that connected young English people in need of work to planters in need of workers. In the England of the middle seventeenth century, finding a place in life could be difficult. The population was exploding, wages were falling, and unemployment was acute. Looking for something better, the resourceful left villages for towns, towns for cities, and some of them took a chance on Virginia.[20]

They were in for a few surprises. Servitude was no lark in England, but it was harsher still in Virginia. Masters were required by law to provide adequate food and clothing (including a send-off of three barrels of corn and a new suit of clothes when the servant's time was up), and they were instructed to keep punishments reasonable. The economic interest of masters, however, dictated squeezing their servants to the limit. By the same token, the interest of servants lay in resisting. This could be dangerous, though, because the master literally had the whip hand. Court records are rife with testimony concerning life-threatening punishments. One young woman was "sore beaten and her body full of sores and holes." Another was beaten "liken a dogge." More than one was killed in the course of a whipping.[21]

Sexual abuse was an added hazard. According to law, an indentured servant who became pregnant was obliged to serve her master an additional two years. Not until 1662 did the House of Burgesses respond to the logic of the situation: The old law encouraged the master to seduce or even rape his own servant or to stand by while someone else did. The new law of 1662 stipulated that the pregnant servant would still serve two more years, but she would serve them under a new master.[22]

Another surprise was that some women servants were set to work in the fields. A popular ballad called "The Trappan'd Maiden: Or, the Distressed Damsel" made the point:

> I have play'd my part both at Plow and Cart,
>   In the Land of Virginny, O;
> Billets from the Wood upon my back they load,
>   *When that I am weary, weary, weary, weary, O.*[23]

Through ballads and by other means, the rumors about the nature of women's work in Virginia reached England. Because proper English women were not supposed to do heavy field-work, this posed a problem for Virginia's promoters. A pamphlet of 1656 offered a neat resolution of the problem: The only English women "put into the ground," it was explained, were those "wenches" who were "nasty, beastly, and . . . aukward."[24]

It was not as though women needed work in the fields to keep them busy. Slaves, servants, mistresses, and daughters carried out all the day-to-day, never-done tasks that made life possible. Every day they ground corn by hand and made it into soup or bread. If their children had milk, it was because the women tended cows. If there were butter and cheese, it was because the women made them from the milk. If there were eggs, it was because the women raised chickens. If there was meat, it was because the women had butchered it, preserved it, and boiled it. If there were vegetables, it was because the women gardened. If there was cider or beer, the women brewed it. While cloth was mainly imported, women did all the sewing, washing, and mending, major chores in a time when work meant sweat and when most people had few changes of clothing. If someone fell ill, women did the nursing; in large households someone was probably sick all of the time. And if the family prospered, chances were that the master would require a new male indentured servant. The women, as a result, acquired another bundle of laundry, another person to be nursed through inevitable illness, and another hearty appetite.[25]

If the woman was married, she was likely to be pregnant, breast-feeding, or looking after a young child. This was a duty and a labor of love. It was also a major economic contribution as surely as growing tobacco or corn. The planters' primary economic problem in the seventeenth century was the shortage of labor. Anyone who brought children into the world, therefore, and nurtured them until they grew into productive adulthood, made direct and essential contributions to Virginia's economic development.

Rearing a child to adulthood, however, was often out of the parents' power. Death was simply everywhere. It came, as we have seen, from wars between colonists and Indians. It came much more often from disease, from what the colonists called "fluxes," "agues," and "fevers"; we would say typhoid, dysentery, smallpox, and malaria. A child born in Virginia had only a fifty-fifty chance of living to see adulthood. About a quarter of all babies died before they reached their first birthday.

Adults were vulnerable, too. Although experiences varied a great deal from one person to the next, we can reconstruct the life of a typical white woman. She was twenty when she arrived in Virginia as an indentured servant. If she lived through her term of service (her chances were not especially good), she would marry almost as soon as she was free. She was now about twenty-five, and she would begin bearing children, one every two years, as was commonly the case in societies without benefit of birth control. Two of her children would die in childhood. Whether she would live to see any of her children grown was doubtful. After seven years of marriage, her husband (who was older) would die, and she would follow in a few years.

Some additional statistics (again, these are for whites) help us appreciate the disruption that death wrought in Virginia families. Only one marriage in three lasted as long as ten years. From the perspective of the children, losing a parent was the normal experience. By the time they reached the age of nine, half of the children had already lost one or both parents.[26] Virginia was a land of widows, widowers, bachelors, and above all orphans.

As a consequence, families hardly ever matched the English ideal. A family, in English theory, consisted of a father, a mother, their children, and servants. In Virginia practice, few children were raised exclusively by their own parents, and many people found themselves raising other people's children. Families were suddenly bereft, then just as suddenly recombined into new households as surviving parents remarried, each bringing with them the children, stepchildren, orphans, servants, and slaves from their previous households. The shape of the family, therefore, was complex, unpredictable, and always changing.

Virginia practice also challenged English views concerning the proper lines of authority within the family, and this was a major step forward for women. In theory, English families were "patriarchal." That is, the husband and father was responsible for the welfare and good behavior of the entire household; he ruled, and everyone else—wife, child, and servant—owed him unquestioning, uncomplaining obedience.

Virginians may have believed in patriarchal authority with all their hearts, but conditions in the New World at times made enforcement difficult. The patriarchs simply did not live long enough. In marrying, for example, young people often made their own decisions; they could hardly ask permission of fathers who were back in England or long since dead. Fathers often realized that their families might have to get along without protectors. Accordingly, the terms of men's wills tended to be generous, more so than in England. Virginia daughters stood a good chance of inheriting land, and Virginia wives were very often given larger legacies than the law required. What is more, the Virginia wife was usually named her husband's executrix— the pivotal person who controlled the property until it was finally handed over to the heirs.[27]

Add in the sex ratio, and the result was a formula for considerable upward mobility among women. Because women were dramatically outnumbered, they could often "marry up." A former servant might marry a property owner, and if she outlived him she might assume control of the property. She might marry still better a second time or a third.

If she was anything like Sarah Harrison, of Surry County, she would have a strong sense of her own bargaining power. When Harrison was married to James Blair in 1687, the wedding ceremony began like any other. Presently, however, the minister intoned the standard question: Did Sarah promise to obey her husband? "No obey," said Sarah. The minister repeated the question. "No obey," said Sarah again. The minister tried yet again. "No obey," said Sarah, one more time. The minister was checked, and the ceremony went on, no obey.[28]

Virginia had its share of Sarah Harrisons, women who were strong willed or rowdy or powerful, women who made their influence felt not only in families but in local communities and in the colony. Nothing in English law or thought encouraged their participation in public affairs. The prevailing idea, in fact, was that women were inferior to men in every way—in physical strength, in reasoning ability, in their capacity to withstand moral temptations—and thus was justified the exclusion of women from voting and holding public office. Yet officeholding was only one way to exert influence. In the seventeenth century Virginia women explored some fascinating alternatives.

The obstacles to female participation in public affairs were formidable. Women were not allowed to vote, to serve on juries, or to hold office in either government or church. This in turn meant that women were seldom drawn out of their immediate neighborhoods for court days and militia musters. Women ordinarily could not read, either. Church was as far as they could expect to go. Consequently, for most women the known world was isolated and small. It was perhaps five miles across and populated mainly by family and a few neighbors.

Within that small world, the challenge for women and men together was to forge some sense of community. In England and in Africa, most people lived in villages. In Virginia, Indians excepted, most people lived on scattered farms; thus for people to form bonds with their neighbors was especially important. Here the Sunday church service was central. So were weddings and funerals, and, when a woman went into labor, she was attended by other women from the neighborhood. Women also served their communities by taking in orphans, paupers, and those who were physically and mentally disabled. In a time when there were no orphanages, almshouses, hospitals, or old people's homes, people in need were taken care of in households. Local authorities recognized this care as a community responsibility; the families who provided it were accordingly compensated by the taxpayers.

Since many of the surviving records for the seventeenth century are court records, we know more about the negative means of maintaining community. Enter the stocks, the whipping post, and the ducking stool—the instruments of public humiliation. Inflicting pain and shame was a practical means of controlling troublemakers in a society with no jails to speak of and with no police force. Transgressors were expected to confess

1. A werowance's wife and her eight- or ten-year-old daughter *(above)*, engraved from John White's watercolor by Théodore de Bry and published in 1590. **Virginia State Library.** 2. Fashioned of mussel shell, silver, and steel, these earrings *(below left)* belonged to Pocahontas according to Rolfe family tradition. Reportedly, she carried the shells from Virginia to England in 1616. **Association for the Preservation of Virginia Antiquities, photograph by Katherine Wetzel.** 3. Charles II in 1677 commissioned this silver badge *(below right)* and a scarlet robe as gifts for Cockacoeske, queen of the Pamunkey. **Association for the Preservation of Virginia Antiquities, photograph by Katherine Wetzel.**

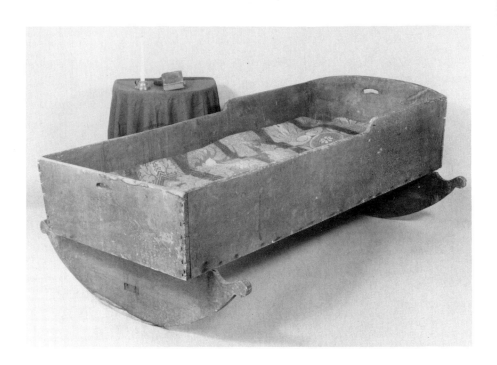

4. Known in Virginia lore as "the Captive of Abb's Valley," Mary Moore was captured from her Tazewell County home after most of her family was massacred in 1786. The Shawnee eventually sold her into white slavery in Canada. Rescued five years later, Moore returned to Virginia at age fifteen and later married and had eleven children. In her old age, perhaps haunted by the experiences of captivity, Moore slept in this large, specially constructed cradle bed designed to cure her insomnia. **Rockbridge Historical Society, photograph by Katherine Wetzel.**

5. *An Overseer doing his duty* near Fredericksburg in 1798, depicted in watercolor by Benjamin Henry Latrobe *(above)*. **Maryland Historical Society, Baltimore.**

6. A slave flogger and wrought iron shackles from early nineteenth-century Virginia *(below)* testify to a harsher reality absent from Latrobe's drawing. **Valentine Museum, Richmond, Virginia, photograph by Katherine Wetzel.**

7. *Above:* Found by archaeologists near River Creek in Poquoson, York County, this fragment of a gold wedding ring (ca. 1650–1675) is inscribed, "Time Shall tell, I love thee w[ell]." **Research Center for Archaeology, Virginia Division of Historic Landmarks, photograph by Katherine Wetzel.** 8. *Right:* A pewter nursing bottle (ca. 1750–1800). Most eighteenth-century Chesapeake women routinely breast-fed their children for as long as eighteen months, and it has been suggested that nursing may have served as a form of birth control. Nursing bottles, also called sucking bottles, were used by women who could not or did not wish to nurse and during weaning. The lead content of eighteenth-century pewter was potentially toxic and in some cases may have contributed to infant deaths. **Colonial Williamsburg Foundation.** 9. Few eighteenth-century doctors were trained in obstetrics, and midwives usually assisted women in childbirth. An exception was Williamsburg's Dr. John Minson Galt, whose London medical training included courses at a midwifery school. Among Galt's implements was this obstetric hook used to aid deliveries. **Colonial Williamsburg Foundation.**

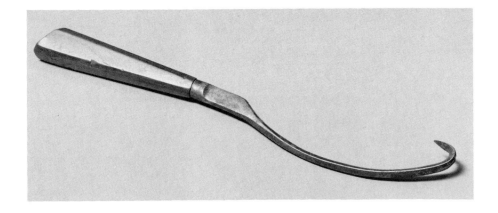

THE MARRIED WOMAN'S
PRIVATE MEDICAL COMPANION,

EMBRACING THE TREATMENT OF

MENSTRUATION, OR MONTHLY TURNS,

DURING THEIR

STOPPAGE, IRREGULARITY, OR ENTIRE SUPPRESSION.

PREGNACY,

AND

HOW IT MAY BE DETERMINED;

WITH THE TREATMENT OF ITS VARIOUS DISEASES.

DISCOVERY TO
PREVENT PREGNACY;

THE GREAT AND IMPORTANT NECESSITY WHERE
MALFORMATION OR INABILITY EXISTS
TO GIVE BIRTH.

TO PREVENT MISCARRIAGE OR ABORTION

WHEN PROPER AND NECESSARY

TO EFFECT MISCARRIAGE.

WHEN ATTENDED WITH ENTIRE SAFETY.

CAUSES AND MODE OF CURE OF BARRENNESS,
OR STERILITY.

BY DR. A. M. MAURICEAU
Professor of Diseases of Women.

Office, 129 Liberty steert.

NEW YORK:
1852.

10. First published in 1847, Dr. A. M. Mauriceau's treatise in favor of birth control remained in print throughout the nineteenth century. The "cult of true womanhood" glorified motherhood, but physical discomfort and fear of death in childbirth clouded many women's pregnancies. **Virginia Historical Society, photograph by Katherine Wetzel.**

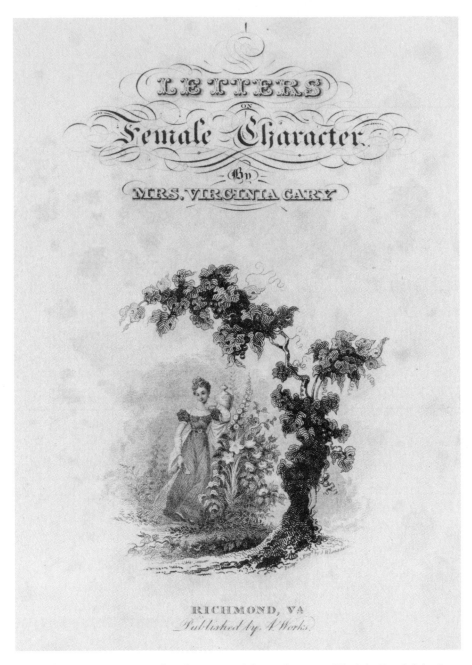

LETTERS
ON
Female Character
By
MRS. VIRGINIA CARY

RICHMOND, VA

Published by A. Works.

11. In her *Letters on Female Character* (Richmond, 1828), Virginia Randolph Cary wrote that "when women are taken out of their appropriate sphere, not only individual, but national misery will be the result." **Virginia Historical Society, photograph by Katherine Wetzel.**

12. Michael Rosenbaum, a German emigrant, and seventeen-year-old Isabella Myers, of Richmond, were married on 30 May 1855 by Rabbi M. J. Michelbacher, of Richmond's German Hebrew Congregation. The ketubah, or marriage contract, stipulated dowry terms and was traditionally read aloud by the officiating rabbi before the wedding and then signed by the bride, the groom, and their witnesses. **Congregation Beth Ahabah Museum and Archives Trust, photograph by Katherine Wetzel.** 13. Only a small piece remains of this wool-on-linen wimple, or Torah binder *(below),* which probably was created by a female member of Richmond's Beth Ahabah Congregation in the mid-nineteenth century. Associated among German Jews with the birth of the male child, wimples were made from swaddling clothes worn at circumcision and were usually embroidered or stenciled. This example shows Daniel slaying the lion. **Congregation Beth Ahabah Museum and Archives Trust, photograph by Katherine Wetzel.**

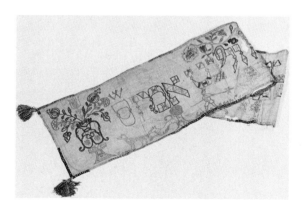

14. Colonel William Heth, of Curles Neck in Henrico County, commissioned this oil portrait attributed to Robert Matthew Sully of his family's beloved slave Sally Brown about 1842. **Massachusetts Historical Society.**

15. This certificate, signed by Thomas Cooper in Petersburg on 18 September 1813, records the marriage of two free blacks, James Butler and Lorraine ("Rainey") Dennery. **Butler Papers, Jackson Collection, Special Collections—Johnston Memorial Library, Virginia State University, photograph by Katherine Wetzel.**

and to beg forgiveness. In the process they reaffirmed the neighborhood's notions about what was right and what was wrong.

Cases of fornication and adultery—the crimes that most frequently involved women—showed how the system worked. Virginians did not as a rule prosecute those who engaged in premarital sex; probably a third of Virginia brides were already pregnant at the wedding.[29] Nonmarital sex was another matter altogether, a violation of good order and, if a child was born to the offenders, a possible drain on local welfare funds. Among the lawful penalties were whippings and fines. A third penalty required each offender to appear in church, draped in a white sheet and holding a white wand. Standing on a stool before the congregation, the offender was then expected to apologize.

Like other systems this one did not work every time. Edith Tooker, of Lower Norfolk, was brought before her congregation in 1641 for the "foul crime of fornication." On being instructed to say she was sorry, she instead proceeded to "cut and mangle the sheet wherein she did penance." The court was not amused; "a most obstinate and graceless person," the clerk muttered.[30] Tooker was resentenced to twenty lashes and, two Sundays hence, to another try at the sheet treatment.

Tooker was getting to be a regular. In an earlier case the court had compelled her to apologize for slander, the other crime frequently perpetrated by women. In early Virginia most information circulated by word of mouth, and personal reputation was extremely important. (Imagine your marriage prospects, your employment credentials, or your credit rating being established by rumor.) Virginia was also a place in which bawdy joking was a way of life. There was a thin line between conversation and slander, and legal actions were legion. In Northampton County, Goodwife Williams called John Dennis a "knave and base knave" and had the satisfaction of seeing him put into stocks for calling her "a whore and a base whore" in return. Edward Drew sued Joane Butler for calling his wife a "common Cunted hoare." Ann Fowler, of Lower Norfolk, was sentenced to twenty lashes and a public apology after she said, in reference to a high public official no less, "Let Capt. Thorougood Kiss my arse."[31]

By 1662 the House of Burgesses was so vexed by the "brabling" women that a new law was passed; each county was required to build a ducking stool to quiet female scandalmongers.[32] (Besides making the offender look ridiculous, the ducking stool held her under water until she spluttered out an apology.) This was testimony to the power of the spoken word. The power to wreck a reputation or to ignite conflict in a community—this was well within the reach of women, and some of them used it to even scores, to intimidate neighbors, or merely to show that they could not be pushed around. At the same time "gossip" could be a force for good. A man who beat his wife, a woman who whipped her servant, might both behave better when they found out their neighbors were talking about them.

Witchcraft demonstrated some of the same dynamics. A witch was someone who used supernatural powers to bring harm to someone else. Everyone believed that witchcraft was real, because it accounted for evil and suffering in a world where scientific explanations were not yet available. In 1671 in Northumberland, for example, Edward Cole's "people all fell sick and much of his cattle dyed."[33] We would look for a germ or virus. Edward Cole suspected witchcraft.

That he accused a woman was no coincidence. In the witch traditions of Europe and Great Britain (Virginia's Indians and Africans probably had their own traditions, but we do not know the details), alleged witches were almost always female. Women, especially the old and poor, were easy scapegoats. For centuries, moreover, women had been stereotyped in the image of Eve—passionate, lusty, and easily seduced by the devil, the culprit who presumably gave witches their magical powers. Actually, a woman who was otherwise powerless might find her only leverage in behaving as though she might be a witch; that way neighbors who feared a bewitching would be likely to treat her with more care.

Or they might take her to court. Virginia seems to have had the dubious honor of hosting the first witch trial in British North America: Joan Wright, of Surry, was accused (and released) in 1626. No one was ever executed for witchcraft in Virginia, however, and the most famous case on record suggests that the authorities tended to proceed with caution. In 1698 and at several times thereafter, Grace Sherwood was accused of bewitching various neighbors. In the investigations that followed, a gallows-happy set of justices could have found sufficient evidence to convict. A panel of matrons found "two things like titts" on her body, the extra nipples with which witches supposedly suckled the devil. Later, Sherwood was bound and thrown in the river to test whether she would sink or float; the spot in Virginia Beach is still called Witch Duck Point. She floated—more evidence of her guilt.[34]

But Grace Sherwood was not condemned. Possibly, Virginia communities were too fragile to withstand the potentially explosive impact of witchcraft convictions. In the Sherwood case the local population was apparently badly divided; when two subsequent panels of matrons were summoned to give evidence, they refused to appear. Were they deliberately protesting the proceedings?

They may have been, for seventeenth-century women did launch into political battles when the occasion arose, and highborn women were involved at the highest levels. Margaret Brent arrived in Virginia around 1651. She lived out her days quietly on a Westmoreland plantation she named Peace, a welcome change after a career in Maryland that had been anything but peaceful. Brent had served as the executrix of Maryland's governor, she had headed off a mutiny of hungry soldiers, and she had asked for the vote—the first woman in America to do so. In fact, she asked for two votes in the Maryland assembly, one as executrix and one in her own right. When she was denied, she lodged a protest against all the assembly's further actions.[35]

Margaret Brent would probably have recognized kindred spirits in the women who were caught up in the turmoil of Bacon's Rebellion. Civil war broke out in Virginia in 1676.

Indian policy precipitated the trouble; believing themselves too vulnerable to Indian attacks, planters on the frontier found a leader in Nathaniel Bacon, Jr., and he began making war on peaceful Indians. When Governor William Berkeley tried to stop them, Bacon's followers rebelled against their government, burning Jamestown and pillaging the plantations of Berkeley's supporters. Luckily for the forces of the governor, Bacon died in the fall of 1676 and the rebellion fizzled soon after.

While Bacon's Rebellion was apparently set in motion by men, women were quickly embroiled, too. One of the most important histories of the rebellion was written on the scene by a woman. Anne Cotton apologized for writing "too word-ishly," but her *Account of Our Late Troubles in Virginia* was in fact an eloquent summary—and it earns her the distinction of having been Virginia's first woman historian.[36] On the side of the rebels were several fiery women. One of them was Sarah Drummond, whose husband was executed for his role in the rebellion. Sarah herself was said to be "a notorious & wicked rebel, in inciting & incouraging the people to the late rebellion: persuading the soldiers to persist therein, telling them they need not fear the king, nor any force out of England, no more than a broken straw."[37]

In this she was mistaken, for Frances Lady Berkeley soon returned from England with a thousand redcoats and orders to crush the rebels. Lady Berkeley was the wife of the governor and well connected at court. When the rebellion flared, the governor dispatched her to England to act as his representative. On returning to Virginia, she continued her vigorous defense of her husband's actions, and after he died in 1677 she harassed his successor unmercifully. She was joined by several influential men who met at her home, Green Spring, to plot strategy; they were collectively known as the Green Spring faction. Eventually Lady Berkeley married the governor of North Carolina (her third governor), but they lived at Green Spring and she re-mained a force in Virginia politics until her death in the 1690s.[38]

From the widow who served as executrix of a small planter's will to the adventures of a Sarah Drummond or a Frances

Berkeley, women in seventeenth-century Virginia frequently assumed positions of power, authority, or trust. There was a catch, however. No matter how well these women performed, their achievements did not undermine the prevailing belief in the natural inferiority of women. Instead, these active women were thought of as exceptions, as honorary men; ideas about women as a group changed not at all.

As the century drew to a close, these ideas were expressed and given new strength by two developments. First was the founding of the College of William and Mary in 1693. The college was for men only and would remain so for 225 years. Then in 1699 a new law spelled out who in Virginia could vote and who could not. While custom prevented women from voting everywhere, Virginia was the only colony to say explicitly that women could not vote.[39] It was the beginning of a long tradition of legislative conservatism on issues affecting women.

As the seventeenth century gave way to the eighteenth, then, some doors began to close on women. For black women, unfortunately, this was nothing new. Their turning point seems to have come in the 1660s. Before then Africans in Virginia had at least a slim chance of becoming free people, and those who were slaves had work routines not very different from those of English indentured servants. But from 1662 on, Virginia lawmakers made a series of momentous decisions: One law after another made slavery more rigid, more degrading, and more difficult to escape.

So far as anyone knows, the first blacks arrived in Virginia in 1619. It is certain that they were brought by force. Less is known about their status over time—whether they remained slaves who were kept in bondage all their lives, or whether they became indentured servants who went free after a few years. Since there was no slavery in England, white Virginians had no fixed ideas about what they should do with their new laborers from Africa. We do know that among the relatively small number of Africans who came to Virginia in the early years, a few did achieve freedom.

An outstanding example was the family of Anthony and

Mary Johnson, of Northampton County. "Antonio a Negro" and "Mary a Negro Woman" arrived in separate ships in 1621 and 1622. They met when they were put to work on the same plantation; Mary was the only woman on the place. How they got free is not known, but at some point they married, and their family life proved to be a miracle of good health. They raised four children, and Mary and Anthony both lived to see grandchildren. Economically they did well. When the entire family moved to Maryland in the 1660s, Anthony sold a 250-acre plantation. Their grown son John owned a 450-acre plantation.[40]

The Johnson family was surely not exempt from racial prejudice. Long before the English had laid eyes on actual Africans, they associated blackness with evil, and they made up their minds that darker-skinned peoples were inferior brings.[41] English prejudice must have weighed on the Johnsons and all other black Virginians.

Still, there was a time in Virginia's early history when race relations were fluid, possibilities were open, and blacks and whites of the same class could expect roughly similar treatment. The best evidence of this comes from the courts' reactions to affairs of the heart. Black couples and interracial couples who were found guilty of adultery or fornication took the same punishments as white couples; in 1649 William Watts (white) and Mary (a "negro Woman" servant) found themselves "standing in a white sheete with a white Rodd in theire hands in the Chapell." Blacks and whites who actually married each other— and there were several documented cases of this—were left in peace.[42]

But not for long. At midcentury the black population was still small—perhaps 500 people in a total population of about 14,000—and the great majority of bound laborers were still English servants. By century's end Virginia was fast making its fateful transition to slave labor. There were thousands of blacks in Virginia by 1700 (between 6,000 and 10,000, it is thought, in a total population of 63,000), and for every new indentured servant imported from England, four black slaves arrived from Africa or the Caribbean.

The legal system was ready for them. From 1662 to 1705 the assembly passed a series of laws that together defined the essential character of slavery and race relations in Virginia. It was a chilling list. Who was a slave? Any child born of a slave mother, the law answered (1662). Indians, too, could be made slaves (1682). Could a slave ever become a free person? Hardly ever, the law answered. An owner who wanted to free a slave would have to pay to send the freed slave out of the colony (1691). In 1723 the law was revised; henceforth a slave could be freed only by special act of the assembly. Could a white person marry a black or an Indian? No, and any white who tried was to be banished from the colony (1691). Could a slave own property? No, a slave *was* property, and any livestock belonging to slaves was to be confiscated and sold (1705). How could a slave be lawfully disciplined? If in the course of punishing a slave, the owner or overseer killed the slave, it was legal (1699). A runaway slave who resisted arrest was to be killed on the spot (1680). A slave who was merely unruly could legally have fingers or toes cut off (1705).[43]

The law, fortunately, was not the only influence on the lives of slaves. As we shall see, slaves themselves continually invented ways of exerting influence on their owners, on the system, and on one another. Yet it is important to appreciate the law's full power. By 1700 the typical black Virginia woman was "chattel"—property—and as such she could be bought, sold, mortgaged, or swapped, or even gambled away in a card game. She would remain property all of her life, and so would her children, who could be taken away from her at any time. She could try to protest, but she did so knowing that her owner had life-and-death power over her. These were among the basic facts of life under slavery, and they would remain in force for more than a century and a half.

2

"Prepar'd for Compliance"

Colonial Women

As the seventeenth century gave way to the eighteenth, life in the older regions of Virginia became more settled and materially richer than before; by the middle of the eighteenth century, Virginia's famous plantation aristocracy was in its heyday. Or, more accurately, it was the heyday of the male half of the plantation aristocracy. Most of the new wealth was created by the labor of slaves, whose standard of living remained at the bare subsistence level. Women of the slaveholding classes enjoyed some of the benefits of the new wealth and presided over increasingly complex households. In other respects, however, the status of white women as a group seemed to have declined: Marrying "up" became more difficult; acquiring control over property became less likely; and compared to what came before and what would come later, women were less visible in the public sphere. When Virginia women found themselves swept up in the revolutionary war, their contribution was essential. It was also quiet, private, and self-effacing.

•

When we think of the Old West, we usually think of the West of Annie Oakley, Sitting Bull, and Jesse James. But there was an older West in Virginia. The westward movement began as soon as the colonists set foot on Virginia shores in 1607. It continued

31

up the rivers of the tidewater through the seventeenth century. In the early eighteenth century the West was the piedmont, and the pioneers were planters and their slaves who pushed out of the tidewater to clear fresh lands for tobacco. In the second half of the eighteenth century the West moved again, to the Shenandoah Valley. This time the pioneers were small farmers on the move from Pennsylvania to the southwest. Tobacco, they found, did not do well, and it was partly for that reason that slavery never became as important to the economy of the Valley as it was in the piedmont and tidewater. Instead, Valley farmers grew wheat, hemp, and a variety of other crops.

The settlers of the Shenandoah Valley also gave Virginia a new diversity of languages, cultures, and religious beliefs. A large proportion of the pioneers were Scotch-Irish, and they brought with them their Presbyterian faith. The Germans were the Valley's other major ethnic group, and they divided into several major denominations; there were Lutherans, the United Brethren, and German Reformed, as well as the pacifist Mennonites and Dunkers.[1]

Because the requisite research has not been done, the experiences of the Valley's women cannot yet be compared with those of Virginia women in other times and regions. However, we do know the frontier made extraordinary demands on women, and some of them rose to the challenge with superb courage. Exploring the border region near North Carolina in 1710, William Byrd II happened upon one Mrs. Jones: "She is a very civil woman and shews nothing of ruggedness or Immodesty in her carriage," Byrd marveled, "yett she will carry a gunn in the woods and kill deer, turkeys, &c., shoot doun wild cattle, catch and tye hoggs, knock down beeves with an ax and perform the most manfull Exercises as well as most men in those parts."[2]

More spectacular were the tales of captivity and escape told by women who fell victim to the guerrilla warfare of the 1750s and 1760s. As Virginians moved farther west, they became embroiled in conflict over control of the Ohio Valley. The English claimed it, of course, but so did numerous Indian tribes and the French, and, as the French and Indian War made plain, all of them were willing to fight about it. After several years of hostilities, the French relinquished title by treaty in 1763. Some of their Indian allies held out longer.

Most pioneer women lived on isolated farmsteads, and for many of them the French and Indian War meant living in terror of sudden attack. For Mary Draper Ingles, a farm wife who lived near what is now Blacksburg, the nightmare came true in July 1755 when a Shawnee raiding party appeared seemingly from nowhere. William Ingles, Mary's husband, was out in the fields and was lucky to escape with his life. Mary was seized, along with her two young sons and her sister-in-law Betty Draper. Prisoners of war, they began a long march west.

Mary Ingles was treated relatively well by her captors. She was allowed to go off into the woods alone to find medicinal plants to treat her sister-in-law, who had been wounded in the attack. She was allowed to carry her sons on horseback, and when they met with some French traders she made herself useful by making shirts from cloth the French supplied. When her captors sent her sons off to be adopted by Indian families, however, Mary Ingles lost the will to be accommodating. She decided to make a break for it.

With an "old duch woman"—a German woman who was also a captive—she plotted her escape. The two of them asked permission to go gathering grapes. So as not to provoke suspicion, they took with them only a blanket, a tomahawk, and the clothes they were wearing. Once out of sight they made for the Ohio River. Day followed day, and the fugitives followed the river, skirting Indian towns, searching up and down for ways to ford the streams that joined the Ohio, looking for the Kanawha and then the New River, which could lead them home.

In time they became "so pushed with hunger that they wood dig up roots & eate that they knew nothing of." Perhaps the strange food as well as the strain caused the German woman to become irrational. Twice she threatened to kill Mary Ingles, so Ingles straggled off on her own. Emaciated, frostbitten, and nearly naked, she at last reached a German farm. She had been on the run for forty-two days. She had traveled nearly five hundred miles.

There were other happy endings. The German woman also found her way to safety. Betty Draper, the sister-in-law, was returned to her family after six years as a captive. One of the Ingles sons died, but the other was returned after thirteen years; reared as an Indian, he would never be thoroughly comfortable in white society again. Mary Draper Ingles herself was reunited with her husband, bore four more children, and lived to be eighty-three.[3]

Hers was a remarkable story, a monument to the fortitude of frontier women.[4] For most frontier women the story was far less dramatic, as they coped month after month with loneliness, drudgery, and one-room living. Visitors from the tidewater commented on the conditions of life in the backcountry with attitudes ranging from amusement to pity to contempt. William Byrd surveyed a remote section of the southside in 1728. At one stopping place, guests and hosts all slept in the same room; "reckoning Women and Children," Byrd counted, "we mus-ter'd in all no less than Nine Persons, who all pigg'd loveingly together." George Washington, who in later life was known for his aloofness, had less enthusiasm for frontier togetherness. While surveying the Shenandoah Valley in 1748, Washington complained of the "barbarians" who "lay down before the fire upon a little hay, straw, fodder, or bearskin . . . with man, wife, and children, like a parcel of dogs and cats."[5]

That gentleman from the tidewater took notice of such things tells us as much about the gentlemen as it does about the frontier: They had come to expect comfort and some degree of privacy. In the eighteenth century in the more settled regions the material lives of white Virginians became far richer than ever before.

The change was most visible in the houses. By the eighteenth century the wealthiest planters were building imposing man-sions of brick. These were not as large as we might imagine, but they were a far cry from the small, wooden farmhouses of the previous century. Nomini Hall, for example, measured seventy-six by forty-four feet, not very big, but it stood taller than any other building in sight and had touches of real grandeur—seventeen-foot ceilings on the first floor, a ballroom, a study, and separate dining rooms for grownups and children.[6] Added to the new houses were all the trimmings—bureaus and bedsteads, tables and all kinds of chairs, mirrors, clocks, tablecloths, napkins, silver, and china.

The average person could never hope to live in so grand a house. Middling planters were making improvements of their own, however. The standard farmhouse in eighteenth-century Virginia was expanded from one room to two, and for safety the kitchen was moved to a separate building out back. While the poorest farmers continued to make do with one room, they nevertheless acquired more goods that would have been considered luxuries by their grandparents. A comparison of two small planters in Middlesex County demonstrates the difference. When Paul Brewer died in 1655 the only luxuries in his possession were a brass kettle and two books. He ate from an "Indian Bowle," and his furniture consisted of one bed and one chest. When John Hickey died in 1710, the possessions he left behind included "two lookeing glasses," "one tin Candlestick," "two butter pots," and "eighteen pounds of best pewter."[7]

Virginia was more prosperous than ever before. To use the language of social science, it was also a place of less social mobility and greater stratification. To rise in the world had become more difficult; poverty was perhaps not as harsh as it once had been, but a person who started out poor was likely to stay that way. In addition, the rich got much richer, leaving a much wider gap between the rich (who made up from 2 to 5 percent of the white population), the middling people, and the poor. All of these developments—the prosperity, the lack of opportunity, and the increased distance between the top and the bottom—can be laid at the door of chattel slavery.

Most obviously, the labor of slaves had produced the new wealth and supported the new life-styles of slave owners, life-styles that ranged from comfortable (by eighteenth-century standards) to opulent. Less obvious was the effect that the slave system had on the less well-to-do. Slaves were expensive, at least double the price of indentured servants, and planters who could not afford the initial investment were left by the wayside. Planters who plunged all their savings into one slave or two might profit, but they might also lose everything; one epidemic could wipe out their labor force and their entire investment.

The wealthy planter, one who could invest heavily and absorb a few losses, stood to gain the most from slavery. In 1750 about half of the white heads of households in eastern Virginia owned one or more slaves. The rest, if they owned land, did well to hang on to it. If they worked as indentured servants or tenants on someone else's land, they had very little chance of ever breaking into the landowning group. With no hope of amassing enough capital to buy slaves, small planters used their modest earnings to buy the trappings of gentility—candlesticks, some pewter, or a butter pot.[8] And they watched while the gentry built mansions of brick.

Such was the impact of slavery as an economic system. The impact of slavery as a human experience is far more difficult to comprehend. Almost all the information we have on slavery in the eighteenth century comes from the writings of white men, and these are few and biased. Some facts do emerge, however, and they suggest that women's experience of slavery was in many ways different from that of men.

The differences began in Africa: Women were only half as likely as men to be exported in the first place. While this was in part a response to the demands of buyers in the New World, it may also have reflected the needs of the Africans. In many African societies, women were farmers, the main breadwinners in agricultural systems that looked very much like the one developed by Virginia Indians. The Africans who procured slaves for the trade may have been reluctant to let their hardworking women go.

However they were obtained—by warfare, by kidnapping, or by trading—the slaves were marched to the African coast, where they were sold to European or American traders and placed in holding pens. Many would already have died on the long trek from the interior. When enough were gathered, they were herded onto ships. Males were sent below, chained and jammed elbow-to-elbow in spaces so low that it was difficult even to sit up. Females were more likely to occupy the quarterdeck, where there was more fresh air and freedom of movement. There, however, they were subject to sexual exploitation by the ship's crew. This grim voyage was called the middle passage, which took at least six weeks and sometimes much longer. It also took a great many lives. One slave in five died at sea.[9] Another one in four would die during the first year in Virginia.

From 1700 to 1740 about forty thousand Africans were brought to Virginia in this way.[10] They cannot have been prepared for what awaited them. Slavery existed in Africa, but it took many forms. Most commonly, it was an easygoing system; slaves in Africa were ordinarily something like resident aliens— not full citizens but still free to marry, raise children, acquire property, and live more or less like their free neighbors.

The first thing the newcomers learned about slavery in Virginia was that, male or female, they would be put into the fields to work. This may have been unsettling at first for the men, who were likely to regard farming as women's work. The second thing they learned was that if they crossed their owners or overseers, they would be whipped. The entire slave system was based on force and the threat of force, and owners came to write about this in a matter-of-fact way. "Made Jemmy whip Easther & Easther whip Jemmy for their having quarrelled some time ago," a Prince George plantation mistress noted in her diary. In the diary of William Byrd, notations of whippings were a standard refrain. "Jenny and Eugene were whipped," he wrote. "Molly was whipped for a hundred faults."[11]

The newcomer had another lesson coming, one that became painfully clear as she learned more English and had more time to observe the plantation regime: Slave families had no legal protection whatsoever. A slave woman could take up with a man, and she could call him "husband," but she could not legally marry him, and he could be legally separated from her whenever the owner chose. She would probably be encouraged to bear children—more profit for her owner—but her children, too, could be taken away.

We do not know how often this happened. Some owners clearly moved slaves around without a second thought. In 1788 a large slaveholder showed immense tenderness for a kinswoman and none at all for his young slaves: "Perhaps, two or three young Negroe Girls may be useful to your dear little Girls, if so, it will be in my power to spare such, and send them to you."[12] Other owners did their best to keep slave families together, but the system might still defeat them. When an owner died, the slaves were often divided among the heirs. When an owner became indebted, the slaves were likely to be placed on the auction block and sold one by one to the highest bidder.

The assignment of slave women to the fields, the use of the whip, and the separation of families—as long as slavery existed, these would remain common features of slave life. Other aspects of slavery did change over time, however. In the course of the eighteenth century, slaves were increasingly able to build a family and community life that was not under the continual surveillance of white authorities. And for a few enslaved women the work routine became less exhausting and potentially more creative.

The importation of massive numbers of slaves in the eighteenth century had radical effects on Virginia's population, and so did the fact that Virginia's slave population began to grow by natural increase. In 1690 about 15 percent of Virginians were black. By 1775 blacks were the majority in most tidewater counties, and they made up from 40 to 50 percent of the population of the Northern Neck. While this shift had profound consequences for everyone, it was particularly important for the quality of slave life. Slaves had once been scattered about on small plantations—one slave here, two there. By 1750 almost half of Virginia slaves lived on plantations of twenty slaves or more, and networks of well-worn paths connected slaves of neighboring plantations to one another. Under these circumstances Virginia slaves had more opportunity to develop both a community life and a distinctive Afro-American culture.[13]

They were also increasingly able to live in families, especially in the second half of the century when the number of slave women was nearly equal to the number of slave men. While we know very little about the family lives that slaves were able to fashion, we have reason to believe that family ties shaped the ways in which slave men and women resisted the slave system: Men might run away; women more often resisted close to home.

Only one runaway in ten was a woman. The women who did escape showed some notable inventiveness; Margaret Grant (an "artful hussy," according to her owner) got away by disguising herself as a boy and playing valet to a white indentured servant, who himself posed as a free man. Most slave women, however, were mothers. They would not abandon their children, and they could not take them along, although a few made the attempt. Resistance, therefore, took other forms. Women slaves helped hide runaways from other plantations. They appropriated food the master regarded as his own. They lightened their labors by slowing down the work pace, breaking implements, and faking illness. They resisted, too, by insisting on an autonomous community life: They made unauthorized visits to nearby plantations; they stole into the woods for secret religious services and social gatherings. Every once in a while—often enough to keep owners in a state of apprehension—a woman slave resorted to direct retaliation, to arson or to poisoning her owner, both of which were easy to do and difficult to detect.[14]

A slave woman might also try to improve her position by lobbying for a less strenuous work assignment. With the growth of cloth production, her chances of succeeding increased. As the eighteenth century progressed, women all over Virginia took up the manufacture of linen and wool. They worked at home and started from scratch with the carding. They spun the yarn, knitted it into garments, and some wove it into cloth. In the prerevolutionary ferment, Americans boycotted imports from Britain, and home manufactures became all the more important. Large planters diverted women workers from fields to spinning rooms. In 1775, for example, Robert Carter ordered his overseers to "sett a part, Ten black Females the most Expert spinners belonging to me—they to be Employed in Spinning, solely." Carter set six more women to spinning a year later. Advertisements affirmed the value of the women's skills: "To be SOLD," read a typical ad, "A YOUNG mulatto woman who is an excellent spinner on the flax wheel, a good knitter, can cut out and make up linen as well as any servant in Virginia."[15]

The young woman may have found spinning monotonous, but she was a seamstress as well, and in this, perhaps, she had rein for creativity and imagination. Women in the eighteenth century produced two types of needlework: plain or household sewing and specialized ornamental stitching known as fancy work. The latter was taught in the schools for young ladies, which sprang up in Virginia's larger towns after 1750. The proprietresses, usually European emigrants, instructed their charges in the polite and genteel accomplishments of the day—a little French, dance steps, drawing, and skill with a needle.

Plate 17 shows an elaborate needlework picture created by Elizabeth Boush in E. Gardner's school in Norfolk between 1768 and 1769. Probably working from an engraving, Elizabeth used as her primary stitch a tent stitch (requiring thirty-nine to forty stitches to the inch) to depict the Biblical story of the sacrifice of Isaac. Gardner specialized in fancy stitchery and taught her pupils not only tent stitching but Irish stitch (bargello), Dresden work (a combination of lace and embroidery), and Queen's stitch, among the most complicated of all embroidery stitches. The school also offered lessons in other polite arts such as waxwork and shellwork, artificial flower making, French, and "other Embellishments necessary for the Amusement of Persons of Fortune who have taste."[16]

The fact that Virginia women achieved so much with their needles is a tribute to their ingenuity. It is, at the same time, a reminder that they lacked other options. In eighteenth-century Virginia, domestic life was the one avenue through which most women could hope to achieve some small distinction. "I have a great and longing desire to be very notable," wrote one Virginia woman. "I'm the picture of bustling notability," wrote another.

Both were talking about housewifery.[17] Neither could aspire to an office in the church or in the government, to a classical education, or to a profession. While this was nothing new, the eighteenth century brought new pressures to be meek and submissive, even within the family circle. For all the increased richness of material life, white women probably experienced less personal freedom than their grandmothers had a hundred years before.

Notability on the domestic front was no mean achievement. While women in the eighteenth century continued to do their daily rounds of essential, life-sustaining duties, the tasks themselves became more complex. Cooking is a good example. The wife of a poor planter in the seventeenth century boiled everything together willy-nilly in the same pot. By the eighteenth century she was likely to have acquired a skillet and a spit, and the culinary possibilities multiplied accordingly.

On large plantations dinner was elevated to high ritual, and the menus were remarkable. The diary of a plantation mistress gives us some idea of the spread: "For dinner boil'd a ham, goose, turkey, tongue, turtled head, pigeon pye, saucege & eggs, vegetables, mince pye, jelly, custards, plumbs, almonds, nuts, apples, &c." On another day she recorded, "Dined on drest turtle, cold turkey, rost beef, stued fish, tongue, sturgeon cutlets, citron pudding, potatoe pudding, cheese-cakes, custards, plenty of asparagus every day."[18] Given the new standards of mealtime elegance, it was no wonder that booksellers began to do a brisk trade in English cookbooks. The books, in turn, indicate the range of concerns that fell within the cook's domain. One of the most popular, Hannah Glasse's *The Art of Cookery: Made Plaine and Easy,* included a "certain cure for the bite of a mad dog," "a receipt against the plague," and instructions on "how to keep clear of buggs."[19]

As Virginia grew richer, then, women's work became more— not less—demanding. The slave woman who was assigned to the fields (and even at the end of the century, 80 percent of slave women were field hands) worked hardest of all. After a sunup-to-sundown day of gang labor, she still had to cook for her family, and the next day she would be up before dawn to make breakfast. But no woman was exempt from labor. Wealthy women escaped the most strenuous jobs—laundry, for example, which they consigned to slaves—but the larger the household, the greater the mistress's supervisory charges. Meanwhile, both slave and free women could expect to bear from six to nine children, and that was only an average. The "innumerable wants" of her household, a planter's wife wrote in 1785, had her "almost in a State of vegitation."[20]

When a woman did achieve notability as a housewife, she herself would probably be the last to acknowledge it. In the eighteenth century the literate women of Virginia had the benefit of books, most of them published in England, telling them how to behave. The message was always the same: Modesty and delicacy were the essential female virtues. In 1770 Mary Ambler copied out a sermon for her daughter's improvement. By combining "natural softness" with "christian meekness," she wrote, "you will not be in danger of putting your-selves forward in company, of contradicting bluntly, of asserting positively, of debating obstinately, of affecting a superiority to any present, of engrossing the discourse, of listening to yourselves with apparent satisfaction, of neglecting what is advanced by others, or of interrupting them without necessity."[21]

Modesty had a sexual meaning as well. Philandering was considered normal behavior for men, but a young woman of the gentry could wreck her life with a single sexual encounter. Virginians were serious when they spoke of the "fate worse than death." In their letters to one another, Mildred Smith and Betsy Ambler returned with horrified fascination to the fate of their friend Rachel, who had been seduced and abandoned by a French army officer. "She is—Oh how shall I repeat, she is indeed lost to every thing that is dear to Woman," Mildred wrote. Eventually, when her son was ten, Rachel married a poor man of the neighborhood. In the meantime she was ostracized and her family was mortified.[22]

Once a woman made it safely to the altar, the emphasis

changed. For married women the key word was obedience. *The Lady's New Year's Gift, or, Advice to a Daughter* put it bluntly. "You must first lay it down for a Foundation in general, That there is *Inequality* in the *Sexes,* and that for the better Oeconomy of the World, the *Men,* who were to be the Law Givers, had the better share of *Reason* bestow'd upon them; by which means your Sex is the better prepar'd for . . . *Compliance.*" "Read often the Matrimonial Service," the *Virginia Gazette* chimed in, "and overlook not the important word OBEY." Thomas Jefferson phrased it more delicately. "The happiness of your life depends now on the continuing to please a single person," he told his newlywed daughter, "to this all other objects must be secondary." No matter how undeserving the husband might prove to be—lecher or drunk, skinflint or scoundrel—it was the duty of the wife to defer to him, quietly making the best of it.[23]

The patriarchal ideal, in other words, was very much intact, and it was expressed not only in literature but in law as well. The law that governed women was the English common law, brought over with the first colonists and retained without major changes until after the Civil War. Under the law, single women and widows suffered no special disadvantages; they had the same rights and obligations as men. For married women it was entirely different. The moment a woman married, she surrendered everything to her husband. He decided where they would live. He was legally responsible for her behavior (if she committed a crime in his presence, he was liable), and accordingly he was permitted to "chastise" her within certain limits; wife beating was legal as long as the switch was no thicker than a man's thumb.

The husband had absolute custody and control of the couple's children. He assumed ownership of the wife's property, her services, and her earnings. Since she could own no property, she could make no property transactions. She could not make a will; she could not pursue a court case in her own name; she could not buy, sell, or liberate a slave. Neither could she make transactions for anyone else; she could not serve as an executrix or a legal guardian. The term for all of this, appropriately, was "civil death."

In the best case the wife was legally passive. In the worst she was extremely vulnerable. If her husband sank into debt, her property could be taken and sold to pay his creditors, and there was nothing she could do to stop it. If her husband was actually malicious, there were no legal limits on his cruelty. He could, for example, abandon her, return long enough to collect her wages directly from her employer, and desert her once more, spending her earnings however he liked. Again, there was nothing she could do.[24]

There was no divorce. That being the case, men and women who were miserable in marriage sometimes resorted to desertion. Newspapers were strewn with advertisements for runaway wives (husbands ran ads to get out of paying their wives' bills). Occasionally, a wife would answer with a notice of her own:

> As my Husband *Filmer Moore* has publickly said his Mother would sooner live in a hollow Tree than with me, and has removed me to my Father's House, with Promise to come and live with me until I could be better provided for (which I can prove by divers Witnesses) but since has falsified his Word, and has perfidiously absented, and kept himself from me these six Months, without any Provocation from me *(so that he has eloped from me, and not I from him)* I do here declare that I intend to remain in the Situation he has placed me until he does come and account for the undeserved scandalous Treatment which I have received at his Hands. And as he has forbid all Persons from crediting or entertaining me, I can prove this to be only Spite and ill Will; for I have not run him in Debt one Farthing, nor removed from my Station wherein I was placed by him.
>
> ELIZABETH MOORE[25]

No matter how sharp her comeback, however, the wife was the one left vulnerable by a fractured marriage. Responsible in fact for her own livelihood, she had no legal control over property or earnings. Susannah Cooper, of New Kent, explained the problem in a petition of 1744. Susannah was married to one Isles Cooper in 1717. She brought property to the marriage. He brought none, and when he deserted her three years later, her property was taken to pay his debts. After many years of struggle, Susannah Cooper managed to accumulate some property. But as a married woman she could not sell it. When her tenants refused to pay the rent, she could not take them to court. And she had no capacity to leave her hard-won assets to her son by will.[26]

Susannah Cooper was an unusually resourceful person, and she talked the General Assembly into passing a special law allowing her to exercise property rights. Had she behaved with proper meekness and modesty, she would never have gotten so far. This raises a crucial question: To what extent did real-life women conform to their passive, retiring image? The answer would seem to be that women in the eighteenth century had fewer opportunities for self-assertion than they had in the seventeenth. In life, as in law, restrictions were more numerous than rights.

Some of the restrictions were physical—and fashionable. In the long annals of fashion, the seventeenth century had been an unusually sensible century. The stiff ruffs and tight bodices of the Elizabethan era were replaced by noncramping gowns that fell to the ground in loose folds. Hair was done simply as well, pulled back from the forehead with ringlets about the neck. In the eighteenth century, however, when a well-to-do woman was "dressed," she could forget breathing freely, walking normally, or moving suddenly. First came tight lacing, a species of torture visited even on young girls. Small waists were in vogue, and corsets with bone stays and drawstrings did the job. Then there was the hoopskirt, heavy and stiffened with whalebone. At times, hoopskirts were a full six feet in diameter, with obvious consequences for negotiating doorways, stairways, and carriages. Hairstyles rose and fell in the course of the eighteenth century. When they were high, in the early part of the century and again in the 1770s, they were very, very high, towers of hair swept straight up from the head, arranged over wires and pads, frizzed, greased, and ornamented with feathers, jewels, ribbons, or beads.[27]

All of this met with a certain amount of ridicule from the press, ribbing that fashionable women probably took with good grace. Jibes at their attempts to become educated were more serious. Eliza Custis once ventured to say she "thought it hard they would not teach me Greek and Latin because I was a girl— they laughed and said women ought not to know those things, and mending, writing, Arithmetic, and Music was all I could be permitted to acquire." Eliza's stepfather then terminated her relatively advanced education, observing along the way that she was "an extraordinary child & would if a *Boy,* make a Brilliant figure."[28]

Eliza was one of the lucky ones. Among slaves hardly anyone had the chance to learn to read and write; Margaret Grant, the "artful hussy" who got away, was one of the few who did. Among free women the illiteracy rate in the eighteenth century was at least 50 percent.[29] Still, Eliza Custis had cause to feel deprived, for the educational system was discriminatory at every level. A boy stood a much better chance than his sister of learning to read, of being tutored, of being sent to school, of being kept there for a significant length of time. Colleges were still for men only. While schools for girls were opened in considerable numbers after midcentury, none of them offered more than the standard fare of the three R's, dancing, fine needlework, and perhaps French.[30]

Every so often, a woman did slip through the system and acquire impressive learning, usually by a combination of tutoring and self-education. The intellectual attainments of Jean Lady Skipwith, of Mecklenburg County, were indicated by the size of her library. She collected more than eight hundred volumes, one of the great libraries in colonial America. Significantly absent from her collection was the best-selling *A Father's Legacy to His Daughters.* "If you happen to have any learning," the *Legacy* warned, "keep it a profound secret, especially from the men, who generally look with a jealous and malignant eye on a woman of great parts and a cultivated understanding."[31]

The dearth of options in education did nothing for women's

economic status, which seems to have declined in the eighteenth century. Girls could learn from their mothers most of what they needed to know to be notable housewives. But when widowhood struck—and it could strike at any time—they were poorly prepared to defend their interests in the outside world. Eliza Carrington, widowed for the second time, was overwhelmed by the challenge of going it alone:

> Oh what a prospect of wretchedness lies before me. The only possible chance I have for pecuniary means of living depends upon my immediately administring upon my Husbands Estate . . . but how or when I shall be fit to engage in such a business [ap]pears impossible to say. . . . This timid temper of mine, so long [indul]ged by the best of Men now left to struggle alone— what will [become] of me.[32]

Martha Washington recognized the problem. In 1794 she wrote to her widowed niece, urging her to manage her property herself: "If you doe not no one else will," she counseled, adding in the creative spelling of the day, "A dependance is I think a wrached state and you will have enogh if you will mannage it right."[33]

Men, however, were making it more difficult for their widows to assume control of property. In the eighteenth century the terms of women's inheritance worsened in three ways. Daughters were less likely than they had been a century earlier to be given land. Second, eighteenth-century wills more often directed that the widow's portion be reduced if she remarried. Third, eighteenth-century wives were less often named their husbands' executrices.[34]

The widow's dilemma was sharpened by the fact that remarriage was becoming a less feasible alternative than in the seventeenth century. The sex ratio evened out in the eighteenth century, and one consequence was that it became much more difficult to marry "up." Another was that it became more difficult for widows, particularly older widows, to marry at all. And outside of marriage, a woman had a very hard time making a decent living. A "wrached state" of dependence was too often the result. The county welfare rolls, filled in the seventeenth century by orphaned children, were swelled in the eighteenth century by women.[35]

There were exceptions to this dismal picture, however. Some widows learned quickly in the school of hard knocks, and, particularly in the towns, women could become skilled in merchandising and in the trades. Virginia towns were still small, even by eighteenth-century standards. In 1790 there were only 3,761 people in Richmond. Norfolk, Petersburg, and Alexandria had fewer than 3,000 each. These were Virginia's largest cities.[36] Even though they were small, the towns offered the best opportunities for women.

A late-eighteenth-century visitor to a Virginia town would expect to find a number of women in business for themselves. There were milliners, highly skilled women who made hats and headpieces, while mantua-makers specialized in cloaks and dresses. There were midwives. While doctors had begun to advertise their services as "man-midwives," childbirth remained in the hands of women, as it had for centuries. The best of the midwives kept busy. By the time Williamsburg's Catherine Blaikley died at the age of seventy-six in 1771, she had "brought upwards of three Thousand Children into the World."[37]

When a theater troupe came to town, there were actresses. There were brothel keepers, too, although because they did not advertise and the local authorities generally let them be, we know very little about them. And there were teachers. Long before the establishment of public school systems, enterprising women offered instruction for a fee to girls and small boys.

Taverns and inns—ordinaries they were called—were routinely run by women in both town and country. Ordinaries were closely regulated by local authorities whose duties included setting fair prices for essential goods and services. In 1770 the Botetourt County Court fixed the rates for taverns: "For a warm diet with small beer, nine pence; for cold diet with small Beer, six pence; for lodging in clean sheets, one in a bed, six pence; if two in a bed, three pence and three farthings; if more than two, nothing."[38]

Local authorities also required innkeepers to be licensed, although they had trouble enforcing the law. Just about anyone could start up a small-time grogshop or tippling house, and women took advantage of the opportunity. In Petersburg, for example, there were twice as many unlicensed women innkeepers as licensed ones; women made up a third of the dealers in the illegitimate liquor trade, the business that, except for millinery and prostitution, engaged a higher proportion of women than any other. The point is not that women relished breaking the law. The point is that the businesses most accessible to women were those in which the stakes were small—low-prestige operations requiring little capital and few skills.[39]

Breaking into more prestigious businesses—those ordinarily conducted by men—was more difficult. One method was to diversify, to parlay a traditional female occupation into something more extensive. Milliners, who were generally the wealthiest of Virginia's businesswomen, were in the best position to try this; they often added dry goods to their lines of hats. Mary Cranmer advertised, among other things, snuff, schoolbooks, and bird cages, and Anne Matthews stocked fiddles, spices, gunpowder, and pudding pans.[40]

Medicine was another expandable enterprise. Since doctors were as yet unable to cure anything except when they got lucky, amateurs with reasonable success rates had no trouble attracting patients. Constant Woodson, of Prince Edward County, was locally known for her skill in healing. In 1776, about the time her husband died, testimonials to her success with cancer patients began to appear in the *Virginia Gazette,* and the General Assembly voted her £100 if she would reveal her cure. Whether the money was ever paid is not known, but Constant Woodson, "famous for the cures she has made," did very well. In the six years of her widowhood she increased the value of her property by more than £200.[41]

The other way to acquire a "masculine" business was to inherit it. Clementina Rind, the most famous woman of affairs in eighteenth-century Virginia, began as wife of the public printer in Williamsburg and mother of five children. Her husband died in 1773, and although she outlived him by only a year, it was a remarkable year. She immediately assumed publication of her husband's newspaper, the *Virginia Gazette.* Soon after, she weathered a controversy generated by a rival paper (also calling itself the *Virginia Gazette*). Having refused to print an exposé of the conduct of some well-known persons (the "guilty Great"), Rind was attacked for having violated her own paper's motto, "Open to ALL PARTIES, but Influenced by NONE." Rind responded with conviction: The author of the article in question had acted out of a personal grudge and then hidden behind anonymity. "When the author gives up his name," she declared, "it shall, however repugnant to my inclination, have a place in this paper." Apparently Rind had the better of the argument. A few months later the assembly voted her public printer in her own right.[42]

Clementina Rind's talent was great, but another reason for her success lay in the structure of colonial business. In order to learn a trade, no formal credentials were required—no degrees, no examinations, no certificates. Instead, one learned on the job by apprenticeship. Moreover, the learning took place at home, because businesses were located there. Clementina Rind lived in the very building in which the *Virginia Gazette* was published (the present Ludwell-Paradise House in Williamsburg), and this was typical of colonial merchants and artisans.

A wife was therefore able to manage both her household and her children and at the same time to learn her husband's craft. When he died, she could carry on the business without missing a beat. Almost all of the women who engaged in unusual occupations appear to have taken this route. Diana Morgan, of Richmond, was a wireworker and stonecutter, specializing in making the screens and grindstones used in milling grain.[43] Mary Cocke and Sarah Scott, both of Amelia, were millers.[44] Catherine Park ran a tanyard, while Mary Wilson, of Norfolk, advertised expert shoemaking.[45] Mary Lindsay was the proprietor of the Henrico County jail.[46]

The highly visible success of these breadwinning women did not cause their contemporaries to rethink prevailing ideas about the proper roles of men and women. Like the political women of the seventeenth century, women such as Clementina Rind were written off as exceptions. Rind, as a matter of fact, was said by one admirer to have possessed "manly sense."[47] That unfortunate phrase reinforced the notion that sense belonged to men and was only rarely found in women.

For Virginians, male or female, to think in terms of equality between the sexes was virtually impossible. A young woman expressed the conventional wisdom: "I own that we are made but for little things and our employments ought to extend at the furthest in the interiour economy and polacy of the family, and the care of our Children when they are little."[48]

In 1776 when Americans went to war in the name of liberty and equality, they did not have women in mind.[49]

•

At every stage of the American Revolution—in early protests against what Americans perceived to be British encroachments on the colonists' rights, in declaring independence, in prosecuting the war, and in framing the new constitution—Virginia men were in the vanguard. The participation of Virginia women, on the other hand, is very sparsely documented.

So far, historians have unearthed only hints of collective female activity on behalf of the war effort. Well before the war began, a number of prominent "widow ladies" signed an agreement to boycott British imports, and they posted a notice in the newspaper to make their position plain. Another group of women, acting at the behest of Martha Washington and Martha Wayles Jefferson (the wife of Governor Thomas Jefferson), raised thousands of dollars for the patriots by organizing collections through the churches.[50] In Fredericksburg "the ladies" turned out to work in the gunnery and helped make "about twenty thousand cartridges with bullets, with which the Spotsylvania militia and the militia from Caroline have been supplied." And in Williamsburg, advertisements announced the need for nurses: "WANTED for the Continental Hospital in Williamsburg, some NURSES to attend the sick."[51]

For most women the war, like life, was primarily a family affair. For a few this meant going with the army. The hardships of the terrible winter at Valley Forge are well known. Not so well known is the fact that Martha Washington was there, too. For poorer women the motivation for following the army was probably economic; they came along for fear of starving if they stayed home alone. The army needed the women as much as the women needed the army. Armies as yet had no elaborate quartermastering system, and they needed women to do women's work.

In the case of Sarah Benjamin, her husband demanded that she come along. Many years later she described her work at Yorktown, where she "busied herself washing, mending, and cooking for the soldiers, in which she was assisted by the other females." While her husband worked on the entrenchments, she "cooked and carried in beef, and bread, and coffee (in a gallon pot) to the soldiers." One morning there was a furious artillery barrage, intense beating of drums, and then "all at once the officers hurrahed and swung their hats." The British had surrendered. For Sarah Benjamin business continued as usual: "Having provisions ready, [she] carried the same down to the entrenchments that morning, and four of the soldiers whom she was in the habit of cooking for ate their breakfasts."[52]

By the time the British surrendered, many Virginia women felt as though they had been through battle themselves. They had waved off their men and settled in to work on farms and shops. They coped with dizzying inflation, and when the fighting came to Virginia late in 1780, they decided whether to turn refugee or to stand their ground. Mary Bolling was one who stayed put. Placed under house arrest in Petersburg while British officers quartered themselves in her home, Bolling had mixed success in saving her property. She talked the British into sparing her tobacco warehouses and her slaves. Her horses were confiscated, however, and her tobacco burned.[53] Betsy Ambler, on the other hand, feared that her father's life was in danger and took to the roads with her family. "Such terror and confusion you have no idea of," she wrote. "Governor, counsel, every body scampering—What an alarming crisis is this."[54] The destruction was massive. Richmond was burned, as were numerous plantations. Some families lost everything.

Some of the heaviest losses, from the standpoint of the owners, were losses in slaves. In 1775 the British had promised slaves their freedom if they would desert their rebel owners. In the course of the war, hundreds of slaves took the risk. For the first time, a high proportion of runaways were women.

Of the twenty-three slaves who fled Thomas Jefferson's plantation, for example, thirteen were women. While some of the female runaways struck off on their own, many of them took their children, and some escaped with husbands, parents, sisters, or brothers. Five members of the Sawyer family, of Norfolk, who had been divided among three different owners, all escaped and had a family reunion behind British lines.[55] When they could take their children, when they could travel in groups, and when they had someplace to go, then women slaves were more likely to seize a chance at freedom.

The venture was more dangerous than they could have known. Some were apprehended, some were returned to their owners, and many died in camp of smallpox and camp fever. But all of them had caught the meaning of the Revolution and had tried, at least, to reach out for liberty for themselves.

A long time would pass before white women were able to make parallel advances. In revolutionary Virginia we know of only one woman who applied the principles of the Revolution to the condition of women. She was Hannah Lee Corbin, of Westmoreland County. In the course of her lifetime, Corbin did three highly unconventional things. First, in the 1760s she became a Baptist, a bold stroke at a time when support for the Anglican church was still compulsory and when the authorities regarded Baptists as subversives and troublemakers. Second, after she was widowed at age thirty-two, she lived with a man to whom she was not married and with him had two children. Her intention evidently was to preserve her inheritance, which by the terms of her husband's will, was to be drastically reduced if she remarried.

Third, she asked for the vote. In 1778 she complained to her brother Richard Henry Lee, a leader of Virginia's delegation to the Continental Congress, that she was a victim of taxation without representation. Why should widows pay taxes, she asked, when they had no voice in making the laws or in choosing the men who made them? Corbin asked her sister to exert her influence, too, hoping their powerful brother would "do something for the poor desolate widows." Richard Henry Lee answered that he personally would favor giving the vote to propertied widows and spinsters. But so far as anyone knows, the issue died there.[56]

How Hannah Lee Corbin came by her maverick stances we will never know. All the pressure, of course, ran the other way—toward meekness, modesty, and domesticity—and to a remarkable degree it worked. The Revolution in Virginia called forth no political women of the stature of Margaret Brent or Frances Lady Berkeley. Martha Washington, the woman closest to power for the longest time, made no attempt to involve herself in politics. This was partly a matter of personal preference. "We have not a single article of news but politick which I do not concern my self about," she wrote in 1788, and a year later, after she had become the new nation's first First Lady, she wrote, "I think I am more like a state prisoner than any thing else."[57]

But Martha Washington's preference for domestic life was also a product of her socialization and of genuine deference; when she was required to write formal letters, for instance, her husband composed them for her. Thomas Jefferson once remarked that women's ideal role in politics was "to soothe and calm the minds of their husbands returning ruffled from political debate."[58] Martha Washington did this wonderfully well. She was someone who was able to do exactly what society asked of her; she was unable to imagine asking for any other kind of life. Her death in 1802 was a fitting requiem for the eighteenth century.

3

"True Women"

A Wider Sphere in the Nineteenth Century

As most historians see it, the antebellum era was not Virginia's finest hour. After the opening years of the nineteenth century, Virginia lost its leadership role in national politics. The perennial problem of soil exhaustion caused thousands of the Old Dominion's most ambitious people to seek new opportunities in the West. Relative to other states, Virginia lost ground in population, education, and commerce.

But for Virginia women, at least for free women, the antebellum decades brought options, change, and new varieties of assertiveness. For the first time ever, women were told that they were better than men at some things. White women made major gains in education. Both white and free black women advanced as property owners, and despite assurances on all hands that woman's place was in the home, both free black and white women formed countless organizations outside their homes. Women were the mainstay of the churches and the primary providers of assistance to the needy, and in these efforts they developed essential organizational skills. When the war came, they were ready.

•

The American Revolution had given new legitimacy to the idea of freedom. For the majority of Virginia women the impact of that idea would be subtle, indirect, and long in developing. For one group, however, the impact of the idea of freedom was immediate. In 1782 the General Assembly made it easy for owners to set slaves free. By the turn of the century there was something new on Virginia'a social landscape: In the cities especially there were rapidly growing communities of "free persons of color." In these communities women were prominent from the beginning.

The 1782 law was a compromise. Before about 1750 slavery existed in all of the colonies, and no one in white America seemed troubled by it. At midcentury, however, the Quakers, some of them Virginians, concluded that for one human being to own another was an evil. The Methodists came to agree, and so, ultimately, did most of the Founding Fathers. In the northern states slavery was abolished. Southern planters, on the other hand, were highly dependent on slave labor, and they were terrified at the prospect of living in a society in which all blacks were free. In Virginia they concluded that slavery was a necessary evil. At the same time they made slaveholding a matter of individual conscience: The 1782 law made it possible to free a slave by the stroke of a pen.

Revolutionary ideals were sometimes made explicit in the deeds setting people free. A slave named Susannah was manumitted with her five children in 1788, her owner believing that "God created all men equally free." Another owner, "being deeply conscious of the impropriety of slavery," emancipated his slave Gilly and later liberated four others. These owners fervently opposed the slave system, and this may explain why the majority of slaves freed were female.[1] The child followed the status of the mother. To free a man, therefore, was to free but one person. Emancipating a woman in her childbearing years might secure the freedom of generations.

In more isolated cases, male owners, acting out of love or guilt, manumitted women with whom they were sexually involved. This, too, contributed to the female majority among free blacks, as did the availability of jobs for women in the towns. Looking to find work, family, and community, women spearheaded the migration of free blacks from the countryside to the cities.

Women and men together made up free black communities that grew at an astonishing pace. In 1810 Richmond and Petersburg each had more than a thousand free blacks. In Richmond one-quarter of all blacks were free; in Petersburg one-third of all blacks were free.[2]

To many whites the manumission law of 1782 was working all too well. Whites tended to believe that the very presence of free blacks made slaves restless. A slave plot to rise and take Richmond was uncovered in 1800, and in 1803 Virginians received word of a successful black revolt in Haiti. The whites reacted by trying to halt the growth of Virginia's free black population. In 1806 the General Assembly passed a new law: It was still legal to emancipate a slave, but the former slave would have to leave the state within a year or else be sold back into slavery. For a few years manumissions came to a virtual standstill. After a revised law gave local courts the power to grant free blacks permission to remain permanently in Virginia, emancipations increased somewhat. But they never again reached the pace set between 1782 and 1806.

Surviving as a free black in a slave society was not easy, and after three momentous days in August 1831 it became more difficult still. In those three days a slave named Nat Turner led a rebellion in Southampton County. Before they were stopped, Turner's followers killed more than fifty whites. White Virginia at first panicked and then set about making sure it would not happen again.

There was very little that could be taken away from the slaves. Free blacks, however, were made to pay. In the aftermath of Nat Turner's Rebellion, the General Assembly made it a crime to teach a black to read. Black preachers were silenced, and black congregations were not allowed to worship unless a white was present. Free blacks could not carry guns. They could not buy slaves unless the slaves were members of the purchaser's immediate family. Finally, free blacks were subjected to the same criminal penalties as slaves. The right of trial by jury was taken away (except in capital cases). Offenses that for whites resulted in fines were in the case of free blacks punishable by the whip.[3]

The process of legal debasement was carried further by local ordinances. Petersburg in 1860 required blacks to step off the sidewalk to let white persons pass. So did Fredericksburg, where blacks were also forbidden to smoke in public. More effective, in all probability, were sporadic instances of humiliation and harassment. In 1856, for example, Esther Fells, a free black woman of Petersburg, stood up to a white neighbor named Thomas Tucker, who had complained about the noise coming from Fells's house. Tucker gave Fells "three cuts with a cowhide" and had her taken to jail. The mayor then ordered her fifteen lashes more "for being insolent to a white person."[4]

Protest was to no avail. Fredericksburg's free blacks in 1838 pleaded with the General Assembly to let them have a school. The assembly not only refused but passed yet another discriminatory law: Free blacks who left the state to be educated would not be allowed to return. With that, a number of petitioners gave up on Virginia and migrated to Michigan. Throughout the commonwealth other free blacks came to the same conclusion. Some moved to the free states, while others colonized Liberia on the west coast of Africa. In the process Virginia lost some of its most aspiring people.[5]

Those who stayed in Virginia did remarkably well, considering the odds. Except for laws regulating the purchase of slaves, the legislature never took away the right of free blacks to acquire, own, and dispose of property. Throughout the antebellum years free blacks made steady progress in acquiring land. And women shared fully in that achievement. In Petersburg, for example, women in 1860 made up 45 percent of all free black real estate owners.

These gains were especially impressive given the fact that most newly emancipated free blacks started out with nothing. White emancipators expected their former slaves to fend for themselves. One of them said it outright in 1802 when he freed forty-two-year-old Sally, "whom I have reason to believe is an honest woman, and one that will earn by her labour a proper support for herself." Young children were often freed along with their mothers; most free black women could therefore count on having to support children. Because free black women outnumbered free black men by a ratio of three to two, the typical woman could not expect to have a free husband helping her out. Moreover, many free black women chose not to marry even when they had the chance; women so recently freed did not give up their legal autonomy lightly. All of these factors contributed to the fact that women headed a very high proportion—in Petersburg, more than 50 percent—of free black households.[6]

Some of these women found unusual work. Phebe Jackson was a cupper and leecher, a nurse who specialized in drawing blood. Amelia Gallé ran a bath house. "HEALTH," she advertised, "Purchased Cheap!" Sally Scott owned an orchard in Isle of Wight; Mary Savoy was a grocer in Alexandria; and Fortune Thomas of the town of Halifax was a confectioner. "In fact," said a petition presented to secure her continued residence in Virginia, "she has been earnestly assured by the ladies that they can in no measure dispense with her assistance and that no party or wedding can well be given without great inconvenience should her shop be broken up and discontinued."[7]

Most jobs available to black women, however, paid very little. While a number of skilled crafts were open to black men, the women generally had to settle for domestic work, laundry, sewing, or stemming tobacco. From their miserable wages they saved to buy others out of slavery. About a third of all slaves emancipated after 1806 were emancipated by free blacks, and about half of the slaves emancipated by blacks were emancipated by women.

The outstanding emancipator in Virginia was Petersburg's Jane Minor. Born a slave, Jane Minor—or Gensey Snow as she was called in slavery—was manumitted in 1825 for her "most unexampled patience and attention in watching over the sick beds of several individuals of this town." Once free she changed her name and continued her practice as Petersburg's most respected nurse. In 1838 she emancipated her first slaves. Before her career was over, she had freed a total of sixteen slaves, all of them women and children.[8]

The Revolution's legacy to free black women was an ambiguous sort of freedom. They were dogged by poverty. They were constrained by dozens of legal restrictions. But they *were* sprung from slavery; they worked hard to spring others; they were self-supporting and often supported children, too; they ran households; and they often avoided matrimony, thereby avoiding legal bondage to men.

We can only wonder what they thought as they observed white women working out their own ambiguous new freedom. Liberty and equality, clearly, were not yet applicable to relations between the sexes. White women nevertheless found new uses for the prevailing political theory. In the early years of the nineteenth century, they listened to ideas about republics and virtue, they hitched these ideas to their profound desire for learning, and they used these ideas to justify their first steps into the public sphere.

Women of Fredericksburg showed how it was done. In 1803 they banded together to found a boarding school for the daughters of the poor. Wanting to hold a lottery to raise the money, they needed the approval of the General Assembly. Here is how they made their case:

> When Your Petitioners observe the Sedulous and Commendable Care which you Exhibit in the Education of the Young of your own sex, when they every day hear you declare that Ignorance is the bane and Knowledge and Virtue the life of Free Government and of Human Happiness, they cannot help saying to themselves that surely the Mothers of free men from whom the Infant mind receives its first and most lasting impressions should not be left to pine in Ignorance but should be made capable of discharging the duties attached to the important Station which they hold in Society.[9]

"The Mothers of free men"—this was the key phrase in that very long sentence. Much as Virginia women may have wanted education for its own sake, the argument that succeeded was a political one. Republics were fragile and could survive only if citizens (male) were virtuous. Sons could grow up to be virtuous only if they were rightly trained in their early years. Mothers were in charge of that training. In order to train their sons, finally, women had to be educated.

For the sake of men and the nation, white Virginians opened the nineteenth century with a new enthusiasm for female education. In almost every town, well-to-do women organized schools and orphanages for impoverished girls. Fredericksburg women organized in 1803, Norfolk women in 1804, Richmond women in 1805, Petersburg women in 1811, and Alexandria women in 1812. In every case they intended to educate their charges and prevent them from having to resort to prostitution. Each of their girls, they hoped, would be launched into adult life armed with basic literacy, Christian morality, and a marketable skill.[10]

As the decades passed, Virginia women continued to organize on behalf of the poor. They built schools and orphanages. They established needlework shops for poor women. They reached out to the needy through religious institutions; members of the Ladies Hebrew Association of Richmond organized in 1849 to support sick and elderly members of their own congregation, and so did churchwomen throughout the state.[11]

The significance of this is not to be missed. In the colonial period the local authorities took it as a given that they should support their indigent people. After the Revolution, however, a new freedom was introduced: the freedom to starve. Local governments in the nineteenth century became tightfisted in the extreme. The poor, the vast majority of whom were women and children, could not rely on any form of governmental assistance, and the need grew acute during the nineteenth century's dreadful economic depressions. While governments retrenched, women saw the want and went to work. For innovation, dedication, and persistence in the field of social welfare, women were definitely in the vanguard.

These organizing women also insisted on more rigorous schooling for their own daughters. Schools for young women were springing up all over Virginia, and after about 1815 their principals (some women, some men) began advertising enriched curricula. In Williamsburg a professor at the College of William and Mary announced that he would moonlight at the Williamsburg Female Academy, conducting the "young ladies . . . through certain *Mathematical, Astronomical, and Philosophical branches*." In Petersburg a Mrs. Barbour promised to teach "orthography, reading, writing, grammar, composition, belle lettres, geography, natural history, history of nations, chronology, natural philosophy and chemistry."[12]

The claims grew grander as time went on. When educational promoters in Buckingham County opened a new school in 1837, they called it the Female Collegiate Institute and in so doing indicated their intention to provide instruction on the college level. By the 1850s a number of schools were calling themselves colleges. "It is our aim," one of the new schools proclaimed, to teach students "to THINK—to reason, investigate, compare, methodize, and judge."[13]

There is no doubt that the best of these institutions were demanding. In 1858 a student in Richmond's Southern Female Institute reported to her parents that she had survived a six-hour exam. "I never was in such a state of trepidation in all my life. . . . I sat from nine O clock until three writing as hard as I could, without getting up from my seat." By the end of the next term, she had developed more confidence. Her geology exam had been "a most searching hard examination," she wrote, but "the best I think that I have handed in yet."[14]

The education of girls in antebellum Virginia was not equal to that of their brothers. But Virginia did go a long way toward closing the educational gap. As Maria Campbell, of Abingdon, put it in 1819, "Daughters as well as sons are now thought of by the fond parent. Education is considered equally their due." What is more, some people began to think that females might have intellectual abilities equal to those of males. In 1822 a small society of young men put the question to formal debate: "Is the mind of man naturally superior to that of women?" After discussion they decided that the male mind was indeed superior.

But it was a close call; the vote was three to two.[15] When the quality of female intellect became debatable, it was a major advance.

Less open to debate was the question of what women could do with their education once they had it. Virginia Randolph Cary, who put her own education to work by writing a book of advice for girls, had a pat answer: "I do most ardently desire to see women highly cultivated in mind and morals, and yet content to remain within the retirement of the family circle."[16] Education was intended to make women intelligent companions for their husbands and virtuous mothers to their children. Young women were encouraged to think no further.

Not surprisingly, the nineteenth century emphasized marriage and motherhood as white women's sole reason for being. But a new variation was struck on the old theme. For the first time in centuries, women were told that they were better than men at some things. "True women," as the phrase went, were believed to be more religious than men. They were also believed to be more virtuous than men and less beset by "animal passions." As one Virginia minister put it, "The attributes of man's nature stretch out their strong and rugged roots toward the earth, for it is in contact with its hard and rocky realities that his work is found; whilst those of woman lift up their graceful stems and unfold their fragrant foliage to the sky."[17] In the nineteenth century the message was repeated thousands of times (and often in botanical metaphors): Woman was first in morality and piety.

How women managed to shed the ancient image of Eve—lusty, passionate, and dangerous—is something of a mystery. But the early nineteenth century was a time of rapid change. In politics the old practice of deferring to one's betters gave way to a rough-and-tumble competition in which increased numbers of white men could vote and stand for office. The economic system changed, too. Canals, steamboats, and railroads quickened the pace of commerce. Factories, built in Virginia as early as the 1820s, revolutionized the pace of production. And there was always the West, beckoning with promises of new riches.

With men scrambling over one another for political power and fast wealth, who would uphold religion? Who would preserve virtue? The answer, of course, was woman. But she had to stay home. Woman was virtuous, according to nineteenth-century reasoning, but she could be corrupted. If she voted, for example, or otherwise meddled in the affairs of men, she would be "unsexed"; she would lose her virtue, and she would take the nation down with her. As Virginia Cary put it in her *Letters on Female Character* (1828), "When women are taken out of their appropriate sphere, not only individual, but national misery will be the result."[18]

Home, meanwhile, was becoming an emotionally richer place, or so ran the new expectations. Twentieth-century Americans take it for granted that marriage should be for love. But it was not until the nineteenth century that this idea was firmly established. Through most of the colonial period, acceptable motives for marriage had included duty, lust, a sense that bride and groom would get along in reasonable peace, and financial gain. Love, if it came at all, came later. George Washington and Martha Custis conformed to this pattern. When they agreed to be married in 1758, they hardly knew one another, and it was not an incidental fact that Martha Custis was one of Virginia's wealthiest widows. The importance of money was underscored by some of the marriage notices in colonial newspapers. When Betty Lightfoot married Beverley Randolph in 1737, the *Virginia Gazette* laid out her qualifications. She was "an agreeable young Lady, with a Fortune of upwards of 5000£."[19]

Practical considerations hardly disappeared in the nineteenth century, but the young increasingly put love in first place. A few days before her wedding, Sarah Anderson asked her diary, "Will Dr. B. be all that I want in a Husband? . . . I would be foolish to expect perfect happiness, but my heart will demand *perfect Love* Love tender ardent and constant." The older generation was more skeptical. They repeatedly warned starry-eyed brides not to expect too much after the honeymoon was over, and they were quick to point out that a marriage could not succeed by love alone. "Love," as Fanny Bernard reminded her grandson, "will not make the pot boile."[20]

But even the cautious elders agreed that love ought to be at the center of family life. The nineteenth century made a virtual cult of the home. Colonial Americans had taken the home for granted as the place where they lived and worked, were born and died, entertained and celebrated. In the nineteenth century the home (the word was often printed in capitals, in italics, or with exclamation points) was increasingly seen as separate from "the world." Actually, the home was set apart, especially in the towns, where family members increasingly left the house to go to school or to a job. In the nineteenth-century imagination, however, the separation was radical: The world was cold and cruel; home was cozy and loving. Anna Campbell recorded the prevailing sentiment in her diary in 1851: "What a happy part of our nature is *the love for home!* the disposition to find there, in that *one spot, all to make* us as *happy as we can be in this world!*"[21]

Women's task was to create that wonderful oasis, of course. Women also were to raise the children, and this, believe it or not, was new, too. We jest about the sanctity of motherhood and apple pie; in the colonial period no one would have understood the joke. Mothers had always been responsible for the physical work of child care. But in the colonial period, motherhood, like the home, was taken for granted, and the real business of character building was assumed to lie with the father. Published advice on how to be a good parent, for example, was almost always addressed to fathers.

In the late eighteenth century this began to change, and by the early nineteenth century motherhood had been transformed into a nation-saving mission. In Harrisonburg the Reverend Andrew B. Davidson told an audience of young ladies that mothers were responsible for seeing that the nation's offices, "both civil and religious, [are] filled with men, sound in head and virtuous in heart. Thus would a people arise," Davidson declaimed, "mighty in themselves, inspiring awe and respect among the nations of the earth."[22]

To prepare young women for the serious enterprise of motherhood, advice writers tried to persuade young women to give up the frivolous life. Davidson condemned the theater: *"Ob-*

scenity," he called it, "*filthy blackguardism*, and *vile blas-phemy!*" He also joined in the national attack on novel reading. Virginia Cary, on the other hand, was a liberal when it came to novels, but had no patience with girls preoccupied with fashion. "The brain which is filled with this wild growth of noxious ideas," she wrote (more botany), "becomes as steril as the field that is left to useless weeds." The Reverend T. V. Moore, meanwhile, reserved for special contempt the life of the co-quette: "Her epitaph and history may be summed up in six words: she ate, she drank, she slept, she dressed, she danced, and she died."[23]

All of the advice writers were adept at telling women what not to do. Telling women what to do was trickier, and this was a problem inherent in the new ideas about womanhood. As yet another minister phrased it, "Females are expected to exert, and actually do exert a powerful influence on society at large."[24] But no one was able to say exactly how that influence was exercised. This was especially problematic for someone like Virginia Cary, whose central theme was that the wife owed her husband absolute obedience. How the woman was to wield power while obeying her husband in all things was a riddle that the nine-teenth century never solved.

It can be argued that the new ideas about womanhood were an attempt to talk women into settling for half a loaf: Tell them they have power in the home, and they will be less likely to want to compete with men in the world. It can also be argued that the new ideas were basically positive: The idea of true womanhood at last gave women credit for doing what they had been doing all along; even if there were no concrete rewards, women did experience a rise in self-esteem. Either way (and both could be true), the cult of true womanhood proved to be extraordinarily durable. For more than a hundred years, every advance made by Virginia women would be made in the name of marriage and motherhood.

Did Virginia's women actually believe the new propaganda about womanhood? Some of it—the "powerful influence" the-ory, especially—they undoubtedly took with several grains of salt. They were very serious, however, about being good mothers. All of the evidence we have suggests that Virginia women, both free and slave, were passionately attached to their children. They tended to be serious, too, about the life of the spirit, and their religious faith was very much a part of their mothering. Not only did they bring up their children as believers, but they also turned to religion to sustain them through the trials of motherhood.

Giving birth was a fearsome ordeal. Emelia Hunter, of Gloucester, said it well in the 1750s: "I am now Every Day Expecting, Either to give Life or lose it—Whichsoever it pleases heaven."[25] One hundred years later women still faced childbirth with the same sense of ultimate risk. By that time doctors, who now attended most births among the middle and upper classes, were using forceps and obstetrical hooks, instruments that made certain kinds of difficult labor less dangerous to the mother.

But doctors were also more likely than midwives to perform internal examinations, thereby introducing infection (the significance of germs and scrubbing was not yet known). Everyone knew someone who had died in childbirth. An early nineteenth-century medical manual published in Richmond listed "Fear of Death" along with "Various swellings of the legs," "Cramp," and "want of Sleep" as normal symptoms of pregnancy.[26]

If all went well during the delivery, the mother was then free to begin worrying about the continued health of her child. She had good reason to worry. Every mother could expect to lose at least one of her children. Eliza Cocke lost two in the space of three days, and to try to cope with her grief she wrote her sister a long letter. Her little boy had been taken with convulsions in the middle of the night. When the doctor arrived, the boy was "bled in the temple artery." Later he was blistered. (Doctors applied skin irritants to produce second-degree burns on the theory that the consequent oozing purged the body of infection.) He died after a few hours. By then his sister had come down with the same disorder. She, too, was bled—through the jugular—and died within forty-eight hours.[27]

Not until the late nineteenth century did medical knowledge

become sufficiently sophisticated to make a real contribution to prolonging life. Until then doctors did as much harm as good, often using "heroic" methods like bleeding and blisters. For their part mothers tried to console themselves with the thought that God's will was somehow being done; "such a dispensation could not have been sent without some wise purpose," as Eliza Cocke wrote. They also assured themselves that their babies were happier in heaven. Slave women, who had to cope with separation by sale as well as by death, shared a common vision of the afterlife: Heaven was a place where there were no partings.

Perhaps the death of so many children intensified women's determination to make good on those who survived. In any case, women took seriously their assigned task of raising virtuous sons and daughters, and they had no qualms about telling their children how to behave. Mary Blackford, writing to her young son in 1841, was full of advice, both specific and general:

> I hope you remember to say your prayers morning and evening.
> . . . Do you comb your hair carefully and wash your neck and
> ears every morning when you wash your face and hands? . . .
> May God bless you dear boy and give you courage, and gentle-
> ness, the union of which forms the charm of the manly charac-
> ter.[28]

As Mary Blackford's sons reached adolescence, she approached them with less confidence. She was visiting the Virginia springs for her health in 1848, when she noticed a great deal of gambling and drinking among the men there. "When I see how the men go on," she told her son, "it makes my heart sink within me to think what a miserable state of morals there is in the world my precious boys have to enter."[29] As Mary Blackford saw it, men inhabited a different world, a world full of vice and temptation. And she was terribly afraid of losing her sons to it.

That, in fact, is how many white women perceived reality: Men were degenerates or escaped degeneracy only by acts of extraordinary will power; virtue was left to women, who were innocent to begin with, who were less exposed to temptation, and who thus had an easier time of it.

Women's roles in the churches reinforced this way of looking at the world. In the white Protestant churches, females were always in the majority, in some churches making up as much as 80 percent of the membership. (For black, Catholic, and Jewish congregations, no figures are as yet available.) Nineteenth-century churches, moreover, spawned numerous organizations, and these, too, were predominantly female. In at least one respect the cult of true womanhood had it right: Women, from all outward signs, were indeed more religious than men.

The Quakers were the first to encourage visible activism among women. Quaker women were allowed to be ministers—a perilous vocation back in the seventeenth century when government officials' duty was to uphold the established (in Virginia, Anglican) church. Mary Tompkins and Alice Ambrose came to Virginia to preach the Quaker message in 1662. They were arrested, pilloried, whipped, and thrown out of the colony. In the eighteenth century persecution was less severe, and Virginia Quakers were able to form stable meetings. Within those meetings the women met monthly to transact their own business. They appointed committees to make sure that women about to be married had thought through what they were doing. Other committees were appointed to attend the weddings; "the aged behaved well," as one such committee reported in 1758, "but the Youth I cou'd wish ware more staid at all such times." The women's meetings also settled disputes, quieted gossip, discouraged slaveholding, encouraged teaching black children to read, and promoted "true plainness."[30]

Not until the nineteenth century were non-Quaker women able to form organizations within the churches; these were called benevolent societies. Once begun, the benevolent movement unleashed enormous energy. Women all over Virginia organized and staffed Sunday schools, where poor whites (and blacks before 1831) learned to read. They formed societies to aid the poor, to buy and distribute tracts and Bibles, to pay for the training of ministers, and to support missionaries.

The central task of these organizations was to finance the spread of the Protestant faith, and they did this mainly by converting their genteel accomplishments into cash. All year long they did fine needlework and other handicrafts, which they then sold at a three- or four-day "ladies' fair." Fairs also featured lunches, suppers, and entertainments; the prize for originality went to the Presbyterian women whose 1843 fair included a lecture on electricity, "in addition to which, the Electrical Shock will be administered to as many of the audience as may desire it."[31] By the 1840s and 1850s, wherever their numbers were sufficient, Roman Catholic and Jewish women were organizing as well. Altogether, they raised countless thousands of dollars.

Women of all faiths also played major roles in raising funds for building houses of worship. As the Good Samaritan Sisters demonstrated, they were careful with their money. When the Gillfield Baptist Church, Petersburg's oldest black church, initiated a building campaign in 1858, all of the organizations within the church were asked to empty their treasuries. The Good Samaritan Sisters, however, held out; "when the Building is in progress," they explained, "we will come up with our mite." A few months later the women turned over several hundred dollars, making good on the promise that the church would see the Sisters' money when the Sisters saw some progress on the church.[32]

Excluded from what men defined as "the world," Virginia women created a public world of their own. They wrote constitutions, elected officers, appointed task forces, raised money, built institutions, and sometimes hired staff members. By midcentury they were expanding the boundaries of their public world. They helped build libraries, they organized domestic arts competitions at agricultural fairs, and they even joined the Sons of Temperance, an organization designed to help men overcome problem drinking. Once again, this did not spell equal opportunity. Men, too, were forming all kinds of organizations, and on the whole the men had more to choose from than did women. Still, for women, organizing was new, and in it we can see a new character of assertiveness.

That quality surfaced in many other ways. It appeared in the lives of celebrated individuals, and Dolley Madison is a stellar example. She was a full generation younger than Martha Washington, and that, along with her Quaker upbringing and her outgoing personality, may account for her relish of public life. Dolley Madison was interested in politics, although she realized there were proprieties to be observed. In 1805 she wrote to her husband, who was then serving as secretary of state: "I wish you would indulge me with some information respecting the war with Spain, and the disagreement with England, which is so generally expected. You know I am not much of a politician but I am extremely anxious to hear (as far as you think proper) what is going forward in the Cabinet."[33]

As a hostess her performance was matchless. During the administration of widower Thomas Jefferson, Dolley Madison acted as unofficial First Lady, and when James Madison became president in 1809, Dolley reached her zenith. She was known, all at once, for being regal, down-to-earth (she loved cards and took snuff), a free spirit (witness her showy clothing), and a genuinely warm and sympathetic person. The combination was effective as she orchestrated the social life that helped turn the political wheels of Washington, D.C. When her husband's second term was over, they retired to their Orange County plantation. When he died in 1836 she returned to Washington, where she throve once again on the bustle of the capital city.[34]

The new assertiveness was visible, too, in the writings of the not-so-famous. Women who wrote letters in the eighteenth century had tended to be apologetic and self-deprecating. Emelia Hunter, for example, had written of her husband's unwillingness to take her along on his travels. "I could assign [no] other reason, but that he must be asham'd of me, I thought he Imagined me Either Ugly or foolish or something, or Other, I don't know what."[35]

Expressions of self-doubt were still present in the nineteenth century, of course, but these were increasingly offset by expressions of self-confidence. Sarah Kemp was sure of herself as a farm manager while her husband was absent. Accordingly, she reported progress in a matter-of-fact way: "We are going on very slow a gatherin corn on the account of its being wet, we have all our potatoes buried about 28 bushels and 15 bushels to feed with, our turnips is very good."[36] Anna Maria Garretson, of Mathews County, wrote to her husband in much the same vein in 1817: "I think I can make out one hundred barrels of perfectly sound pure corn, which I will ship to you provided you can get 10$, otherwise I should prefer grinding it, and then I shall be certain of a good price," and so on for three pages. Anna Garretson was so confident of her own abilities, in fact, that she made a habit of mocking the man her husband had hired as overseer—"your wise overseer," she called him sarcastically, on another occasion remarking, "so much for your great manager."[37]

As these letters suggest, there was an economic dimension to women's new attitude, and when it came to property, the improvement was measurable. While the common law gave married women next to no property rights, there was a second legal system called equity. Under this system a married woman could, if she acted in time, acquire a "separate estate"; that is, she could own property and exempt it from her husband's control, in some cases exercising the same rights as a man. Innkeeper Margaret Falkner preserved her right to run a business by making a contract with her intended husband, James Bromley. Her rights, the contract stated, were not subject to the "interference, interruption, hindrance, [or] participation" of James Bromley or any "after taken husband." The contract worked. Margaret Falkner's property was preserved intact, and when she died in 1814 she left it to endow Chesterfield County's first school for poor children.[38]

There were many obstacles to the establishment of these separate estates, the chief one being the implication that the husband was incompetent. But the numbers of separate estates still grew in the antebellum years. So did the numbers of widows who refused to accept the provisions their husbands had made for them by will; these women then filed for fairer settlements. A higher proportion of free women—white and black—owned property than ever before, and they made more property transactions. They bought and sold more, they lent and borrowed more, and they made more gifts and wills.[39]

Part of the reason that more women were in control of property was that more women were unmarried for significant portions of their lives. Divorce was legalized in Virginia after the Revolution, and although a divorce was very difficult to obtain—until 1827 a special act of the legislature was required to get one—it did present one added option.[40] The single life, meanwhile, was apparently becoming more attractive, at least for those who had a reliable income. Widows, even young widows, often did not remarry if they could afford to remain independent. And some women chose not to marry in the first place.

Whatever their marital status, Virginia women looked to other women for understanding and emotional fulfillment. Virginia Cary, in her *Letters on Female Character,* assumed that female friends, and not husbands, were women's main source of affection. "Choose then," she wrote, "a firm-minded, amiable-tempered, warm-hearted woman." Female friendships were expected to be—and were—romantic: "Oh my dear loved Betsey, (now what would I give if you had a name a little more romantic) how shall I exist without you?" They were intense: "Life seems a dreary waste since deprived of your loved Society." And they were sensual: "How delightful the thought of being again in the arms of my first [and] best of friends."[41]

In sum, marriage and remarriage were less commonplace than before, divorce was possible, female friendship was on the rise, and so were separate estates. For women of the working classes the introduction of factory jobs (in textile mills for whites, in tobacco factories for free blacks and a few whites) meant new opportunities for wage earning. The overall result was greater autonomy for Virginia women, at least in the sense of less dependence on individual men.

Little wonder then that the nineteenth century spent so much effort and ink telling women to stay home and to mind their husbands. A hundred years earlier that had hardly been necessary, for most women had nowhere else to go. By the early nineteenth century, however, some women had some limited choices, and their diaries began to show it. As a young woman, Eliza Ruffin resolved never to subject herself to the "servitude" of marriage, and she heartily objected to the fact that "superiority, authority and freedom in all things" were given to men. Eventually Eliza relented and was married—"matronized," as she later termed it.[42] But she believed she had a choice, and that was significant in itself.

To speak of choices in a slave society is to risk overstating the case. On any matter touching slavery or race relations, the choices open to Virginia women diminished in the three decades before the Civil War. The increasing nervousness of the whites was due in part to events outside the state; in the 1830s northern abolitionists began calling for an immediate end to slavery. But the white South was already on the defensive. As early as the 1820s many influential white men decided to make slavery a permanent feature of Virginia life, and they invented a new rationale for it. No longer bemoaning the existence of slavery as a necessary evil, these men argued that slavery was a positive good, a fundamentally humane labor system that bestowed civilization and Christianity on a benighted people. With each passing decade tolerance for any other opinion grew thinner.

The positive good theory never carried any weight with slaves themselves. The injustice of the system was obvious to them, and one way they withstood it was by adapting Christian teaching to their own needs. Slave religion emphasized the equal dignity of all souls, love and respect for fellow slaves, the promise of deliverance from suffering, and the faith that in the next life slaves and masters would all get what they deserved.

Some masters were better than others, as interviews with aged former slaves make clear. These interviews, conducted in the 1930s, reveal the common qualities of slave life in the 1850s and

1860s.[43] They tell of some good times, to be sure—holidays, for instance, and nights when the patrollers (men who came around on horseback to punish suspicious activity) were outwitted by quick-thinking slaves. But the interviews taken together constitute a thorough indictment of the slave system. The common refrains are sales, whippings, long hours of hard work, and—the special burden of slave women—sexual exploitation by owners and overseers. To make matters worse, whites often blamed this on the slave women. When whites spoke of the "true woman," they were not referring to the woman slave. White men conveniently imposed on black women the more ancient image of Eve—lusty, seductive, and therefore "responsible" for men's lack of self-control.

Resistance was possible but, as always, dangerous. Fanny Berry recounted the story of Sukie: "Ole Marsa was always tryin' to make Sukie his gal." One day he made the mistake of trying to force her while she was making lye soap in the kitchen. "She took an' punch ole Marsa an' made him break loose an' den she gave him a shove an' push his hindparts down in de hot pot o' soap. Soap was near to bilin', an' it burnt him near to death." That was effective: "Marsa never did bother slave gals no mo'." But Sukie paid. After a few days she was put on the auction block and sold.[44]

Sometimes sexual unions between slave women and their masters secured a few privileges for the women. Occasionally, when children were born of these unions, the master would acknowledge his own, granting his children freedom and maybe even an inheritance. More often, the children remained in slavery. Of all of slavery's bizarre cruelties, this was among the worst: Some slave children were half brothers and half sisters of the all-white children who would one day inherit them.

This was the aspect of slavery that stung white women the most. Along with their men, women of the slaveholding classes reaped benefits from slavery—economic benefits, high social status associated with slave ownership, and exemption from the grubbiest forms of housework. But white women's experience

of slavery was different from that of white men, and consequently the women's perspectives on slavery tended to be more
negative.

This is not to say that white women advocated racial equality
(very few would have gone so far) or that they all were
abolitionists at heart. While some passionately opposed slavery,
others gave public support to the theory that slavery was a
positive good. Julia Gardiner Tyler, a Virginian by marriage and
wife of the tenth president of the United States, attracted
considerable notice in 1853 when she published a letter in a
major magazine claiming that the plantation was a civilizing
influence.[45] On the question of whether slavery as a system was
right or wrong, there was no consensus.

Nor was there any single pattern of day-to-day interaction
between mistresses and slaves. Preliminary evidence suggests
that white women were far less concerned with slavery in the
abstract than they were with the particular qualities of particular
slaves. This highly personal approach had variable consequences, some positive, others tragic. On the positive side,
white women who had the legal authority were more likely than
were men to emancipate slaves, to make a financial sacrifice for
the sake of rewarding the exceptional individual.[46] At the same
time, white women had a reputation for inflicting exceptionally
cruel punishments on individuals who crossed them. "Marsa
was a well-meaning man," Henrietta King recalled, "but ole'
Missus was a common dog." When King was nine years old, her
mistress crushed one side of her face under a rocking chair. King
was disfigured for life.[47]

While there was great variation in both theory and actual
behavior, slaveholding women reached something like a consensus on how the slave system affected them. In a word, they felt
burdened. Mistresses were in charge of the household, the
dairy, the smokehouse, the poultry yard, and the garden; they
cut out all the slaves' clothing and supervised the sewing; they
handed out food rations; they nursed the sick. They worked
hard, felt harried much of the time, and hotly resented outsiders
who imagined them to be ladies of leisure. Even more did they

resent outsiders who condemned slaveholding as sin. As the mistresses saw it, slavery was the present reality. If there was any humanity in the system, it was due to the self-sacrifice of the mistresses, who, as one minister's wife wrote in 1859, were "doing all that they can do, for the comfort, and happiness of the slaves, providentially committed to their care."[48]

A few challenged the system itself. Anne Randolph Page, of Frederick County, opposed slavery on religious grounds, and after she was widowed in 1826 she freed all the slaves under her control, paid for their passage to Liberia, and sent along provisions for their first pioneering year. Margaret Mercer, as a single woman, had the right to set her slaves free and free them she did. Her remaining inheritance she used to found a school in Leesburg, where she put her students to work making handicrafts. These were sold, and the proceeds were donated to the Liberia project.[49]

Making a public stand, however, was difficult for women, not only because of the growing defensiveness about slavery but also because of the clamps put on female political activity. Mary Berkeley Blackford, of Fredericksburg and later of Lynchburg, had the remarkable facility of trying to see slavery from the slave's point of view. She freed her own two slaves. She begged and borrowed to buy and free more slaves and to found a school for girls in Liberia. When she tried to promote a petition to the General Assembly, however, she was stymied. A male ally in Richmond assessed the situation: "The *names* of Ladies will not be desirable, as the Legislature may not, probably, appreciate their value. . . . I should think if a gentleman of energy would put a memorial in circulation several hundreds of your most intelligent citizens might be induced to sign it."[50]

Still, there were women who insisted on being heard. One of them was Margaret Douglass, a white woman who was arrested in 1852 for keeping a school for free black children in Norfolk. Douglass was not, in fact, opposed to slavery. But she was appalled at the treatment of free blacks, and during her trial she did not hesitate to say so. She was sentenced to thirty days in jail.[51]

And there were the women of Augusta County, 215 of them, who in the aftermath of Nat Turner's Rebellion petitioned the legislature to abolish slavery in Virginia. "Although we feel all the timidity incident to our sex in taking this step, yet we hold our right to do so to be unquestionable." For the petitioners anything was better than living in fear of full-scale revolt. "Tell us not of the labors & hardships which we shall endure when our bond-servants shall be removed from us," the women said. "They have no terrors for us."[52]

Finally, there was the petition that nine black women—probably slaves—signed and sent to Congress in 1837. They wrote in support of a bill to abolish slavery in the District of Columbia, and they enclosed a cover letter that minced no words. "I hope you good men would do something in this business, but it seems all talk up with you in Congress."[53] It *was* all talk, until 1861. Then the war came, and for a time everything was different.

4

"Never Was No Time Like 'Em Befo' or Since"

The War and After

When Jefferson Davis wrote his history of the Confederate government, he dedicated it to the women of the Confederacy, praising their services as nurses, their "domestic labors," their "faith," their "fortitude," and their "patriotism."[1] Virginia women achieved many firsts during the Civil War, but this was among the most significant: For perhaps the first time they received credit where credit was due. During the war itself and for many years afterwards, Southerners exalted the efforts of their women. As a consequence, we know more about Virginia women in the four years of war than in any other time.

By contrast, historians are just beginning to explore how women fared after the war was over. The single most important fact was that slavery was dead. Black women went to work immediately to make freedom meaningful, especially through education. But they faced an uphill struggle. Virginia women both black and white had made extraordinary exertions during the war, but in the poverty of postwar Virginia they had difficulty translating their wartime contributions into long-term gains. In some ways they lived like the pioneers of the seventeenth and eighteenth centuries: The emphasis was on survival.

•

North and South went to war in April 1861, and for Virginia women the pace of life quickened immediately. "We lived on excitement," one remembered. "To be idle was torture," wrote another.[2] Women who had never before kept diaries began writing down daily events, for they felt they were living in momentous times. This was doubly true for slaves. Many had no choice but to labor for their owners and a Confederate victory; at the same time, they knew that the defeat of the Confederates might end slavery once and for all. Working within earshot of the guns at Manassas, an elderly slave cook made dinner for her owners as usual. But after every volley of gunfire she whispered, "Ride on, Massa Jesus."[3]

All too soon the women's sense of heightened purpose and alertness was accompanied by anxiety and grief. Mary Ann Whittle lost a son in the first months of the fighting. "This dreadful war," she wrote in 1861, "when o when will it be at an end." Beginning in the fall of 1862, black Virginians in Union-controlled areas were enlisted in the Union army.[4] From then on, black women shared the fear for the lives of husbands and sons.

The Civil War made women more aware than ever of the limitations their society placed on them. "Never before did I regret being a woman," Bessie Callender wrote as the troops were gathering, "but now it grieves me to be unable to fight." Kate Spaulding, a Virginian who had married a Northerner, watched with dismay as the country divided. "I feel like a *brass strap* that don't fit *any-where*," she wrote from New York. "If I were a man," she added, "I know where I'd be!" In 1863 when things began to look grim for the Confederate cause, Lucy Breckinridge thought women could help: "I wish the women could fight, and I do think they might be allowed to do so in the mountains and in the fortified cities. . . . I would gladly shoulder my pistol and shoot some Yankees."[5]

While they were forbidden to fight, women stretched accept-able roles to their outer limits. A few of the most adventurous found new uses for hoopskirts and elaborate hairdos: Under crinolines and wigs, smugglers sneaked messages, medicines, and weapons into the Confederacy. Another venturesome few entered into espionage, using their skills as either servants or coquettes to gather classified information.

Belle Boyd experimented with the flirtation technique. She began as a spy when she was only seventeen, making the acquaintance of Union soldiers who occupied her hometown (Martinsburg, now in West Virginia) and sending their secrets on to Confederate leaders. She was caught, but as she was young and clearly an amateur (she sent messages in her own handwriting, using no code), she was soon released. By the fall of 1861 she had moved to her aunt's home in Front Royal, where she became a professional spy, a courier for the Confederate intelligence service. Four more times she was arrested, the last time at sea in 1864 as she tried to run the blockade with dispatches intended for England. This time she was banished to Canada, but Belle Boyd once again landed on her feet: She married the Union captain who had arrested her. Before her life was over, she had a brief career as an actress; she married twice more; she raised five children; and finally she became a lecturer, speaking to packed houses, South and North, about her exploits as a secret agent for the Confederacy.[6]

For the Union side, Virginia's most noteworthy female spies were the team of Elizabeth Van Lew and Mary Elizabeth Bowser of Richmond. Van Lew was a wealthy woman whose antislavery opinions were well known. Bowser had been a slave in the Van Lew household; in the 1850s she was freed and sent north to school. When the war came, Bowser found employment on the domestic staff of the Confederate White House and funneled everything she could learn to Van Lew. Van Lew in turn set up five relay stations to send the messages on to General Ulysses S. Grant. Although she was under surveillance, Van Lew's high social position protected her from arrest, and she did her best to throw the Confederates off guard by pretending she was insane. She dressed eccentrically and went about town humming and babbling to herself. While she depended on Mary Elizabeth Bowser and a network of couriers (some of them Van Lew's servants), both the notoriety and the credit fell on Crazy

Bet herself. Richmonders of her own class ostracized her for the rest of her long life. President Grant, however, appointed her postmistress of the city.[7]

Thousands of women, meanwhile, risked personal danger to follow the army. Sarah Pryor resolved to take her sons and to follow her husband's regiment through the entire war. "I did not ask his permission. I would give no trouble. I should only be a help to his sick men and his wounded." Sarah Pryor intended to stay with the troops even after her husband gave up his command to serve in the Confederate Congress. He, however, had other ideas and ordered her (officially, in his capacity as a colonel) to report to Richmond.[8]

Thus ended Sarah Pryor's career as a camp follower. But wherever the battles were, women were close by. Some (and their numbers probably increased as the Confederate economy deteriorated) engaged in prostitution. The most notable of the alleged prostitutes were Mary and Molly Bell, of Pulaski County, who disguised themselves as soldiers and served for two years as "Tom Parker" and "Bob Martin" before they were found out. They had "adopted the disguise of soldiers," their captain explained, "better to . . . hide their iniquity."[9] If the Bells were indeed prostitutes, a great many men must have helped guard their secret. In any case, any woman who was not the wife of an officer was likely to be suspected of having loose morals. So much the worse for the countless women who served as seamstresses, cooks, nurses, and washerwomen and who never received deserved credit for their contributions.

Not surprisingly, the women who performed services at home were treated as heroines. The army's first need was for uniforms, tents, bedding, and bandages, and because women were already organized through the churches, they were able to reorganize instantaneously as sewing squadrons. Sewing machines were donated by the few who owned them (they had been on the market for only a few years). In the summer of 1861 the volunteers worked ten-hour days and six-day weeks, and when they were not sewing, they were knitting. As Mary

Boykin Chesnut remarked, "I do not know when I have seen a woman without knitting in her hand."[10]

In time, the Confederate government began paying its seamstresses—paying badly, but paying. Marinda Cochran described how the system worked in 1863. On Thursdays she fetched materials at the government depot and brought them home to her farm. Each day, along with her sisters and daughters (five workers altogether), she rose before dawn, did chores, and began sewing; the youngest daughter cooked and did housework, freeing the rest to sew full-time. After a week they took their finished work back to the depot, collected their pay, and if cloth was available, took it home for the next week's work. In six months she calculated they had made "81 large overcoats, 53 jackets, 38 pairs of drawers and six pairs of pants," and they could have done more were it not for shortages of cloth. The five of them together made an average of $10 a week.[11]

Nursing, too, was sometimes work that could be done at home. This was traditional women's work, and untold numbers of sick and wounded soldiers recuperated in private homes under the care of volunteer nurses. Nursing was also a traditional task of black women, and in both homes and hospitals many of the nurses were slaves or free blacks. Service in the hospitals required stern stuff. Phoebe Yates Pember, after two months as matron of Chimborazo Hospital in Richmond, felt like a hardened veteran. "I sometimes wonder if I am the same person who was afraid to look at a dead person, for I have no timidity and hardly any sensibility left. . . . After the battle of Fredericksburg I stood by and saw men's fingers and arms cut off and held the brandy to their lips, washing the wounds myself."[12]

A hospital matron needed executive talent as well as a strong stomach. Phoebe Yates Pember was undersupplied, understaffed, and responsible for the nursing and feeding of as many as seven hundred men at a time. She was assigned to live in a small house "through the planks of which I can see the stars and the snow too" and was at first paid so little that she took in clerical work at night to make extra money. Within a year, however, the government recognized her as indispensable and began paying her a respectable salary.[13]

Sally Louisa Tompkins was another outstanding hospital administrator, and the honor bestowed on her was unique: Sally Tompkins was the first American woman to be commissioned as a regular military officer. Originally from Mathews County, Tompkins had moved to Richmond shortly before the war began. After the first battle of Manassas, she opened a private, twenty-five-bed hospital, which she ran with the help of four female slaves and a number of part-time volunteers. They had worked for only a few weeks when all private hospitals were ordered closed to military patients; soldiers were to be cared for in military hospitals only.[14] Apparently in order to keep her hospital open, Sally Tompkins was commissioned. On 9 September 1861 she was appointed a captain—in the cavalry, no less. "Captain Sally" accepted the rank, refused the pay, and with her staff saw to the recovery of an extraordinary number of patients. Of the 1,333 men they treated, only 73 died.

While nursing and sewing had long been considered women's work, organizing these services and managing them on a grand scale was new for women. They were justly proud of their newfound managerial capacity. Bessie Callender, the same woman who had chafed at being unable to fight, found her niche in supervising seamstresses: "Its a serious job to cut out and distribute and see if its well done, then lastly but not the easiest to pay all the women." This, as she explained to her relatives, often kept her too busy to visit them.[15] This was probably the first time in their history that Virginia women of the propertied classes were able to put work ahead of family.

The war brought still other new work experiences to women. Women were hired as secretaries (or "clerks"), copying out government documents in longhand. Other new lines of work were riskier. The great majority of workers in the Confederate ordnance laboratory, an ammunition factory near Richmond, were women. In March 1863 forty of them were killed in an explosion.[16]

The plant reopened after a few weeks, and new workers stood in line to take the places of the dead. These women may have been patriots, but they were also desperate for paying work. All through the antebellum years, the wages for women's work had been pitiful. This continued during the war, and what made matters worse was an astonishing rate of inflation. Prices doubled and doubled again, and the crisis deepened as the government began impressing goods—that is, forcing businesses to sell goods to the government at prices the government itself fixed. Civilians, meanwhile, had no choice but to pay the higher prices set by the merchants.

On 2 April 1863 women in Richmond took to the streets. For days the newspapers had reported that women in other Southern cities were doing some impressing of their own—demanding that merchants sell them goods at the government price and confiscating goods from merchants who refused them. On 1 April three hundred women gathered in a Baptist church in Richmond. Led by Mary Jackson, a "huckster" in the local marketplace, they decided on an impressment.

The very next day, they assembled in Capitol Square. Before long their numbers swelled to over two thousand, and as they surged toward the business district their anger prevailed over Mary Jackson's calls for measured action. Out came hammers and axes. Windows and doors were smashed, and the rioters made off with flour, bacon, shoes, brooms, and whatever else was to be found in the dry goods stores. The police were in a near panic when a combination of arrests and threats (Jefferson Davis spoke to the crowd and sympathized with the needy, and Governor Letcher threatened to open fire in five minutes if they did not leave) caused the rioters to disperse.

A newspaper later tried to discredit the rioters as "a handful of prostitutes, professional thieves, . . . Yankee hags, [and] gallows-birds from all lands but our own." Cooler heads would have realized that they were ordinary women whose men were off at war, who were not cushioned by wealth, and who were suffering at the hands of profiteers. And while they did not succeed in carrying out an orderly impressment, they did get results: The city council soon instituted weekly distributions of food and fuel to soldiers' wives and others among the "meritorious poor."[17]

Everywhere in Virginia, women were resourceful in the face of economic hardship. They dusted off spinning wheels and looms, conjured up their grandmothers' recipes for medicines, invented substitutes for coffee, sugar, wheat flour, and leather, and then found substitutes for the substitutes.[18] They also worked to keep churches and schools going despite the pressures of war. Hanora Flynn Kelley of Union-occupied Harrisonburg slipped through the lines and made her way to Richmond, where she managed to exchange Confederate currency (soon to be worthless) for gold. With that gold Harrisonburg Catholics acquired their first church.[19]

In most parts of Virginia, teachers barely were able to keep their schools operating on something like a normal schedule. In the Hampton Roads area, however, the war years were a time of educational innovation. Only three months after the war began, the area was home to nine hundred "contraband"—slaves who left their masters to seek freedom behind Union lines—and there were ten thousand contraband in the area by the end of 1863. Both adults and children were eager to learn to read and write, and they were taught largely by missionaries from the North. Their inspiration, however, was Mary Peake, of Hampton. Peake was born free and grew up to insist that blacks be educated. In the 1850s she conducted a discreet illegal school in Hampton, and, when the town came under Federal control in 1861, she rejoiced to bring her school out into the open. She was only thirty-nine when she died of tuberculosis early in 1862.[20]

No amount of resourcefulness, however, could overcome the triple evils of inflation, scarcity, and destruction wrought by both armies. Among the contraband, thousands of women and children were placed in refugee camps, where they lived out the war in great poverty. (Only men were assigned land to work.) On the Confederate side, free black women were subjected to impressment—forced labor in the hospitals or in the countryside foraging fuel and food for the troops. White women on

16. *The Quilting Party* (ca. 1854–1900), artist unknown. Derived from a black-and-white illustration printed in *Gleason's Pictorial* magazine on 21 October 1854, this oil painting depicts a mid-nineteenth-century quilting bee in western Virginia. A quilting bee was an all-day gathering of female friends and neighbors usually followed by an evening of social activities after the men joined the group for supper. A detail from this colorful painting is reproduced on the front cover of this book. **Abby Aldrich Rockefeller Folk Art Center, Williamsburg, Virginia.**

17. Signed "Eliz[abe]th Boush workd this pece at E[lizabeth] Gardners [school in Norfolk]—1768:9," this silk-on-linen needlework depicts the biblical story of the sacrifice of Isaac. **Courtesy, Museum of Early Southern Decorative Arts, Winston-Salem, North Carolina.**

18. Mary Read Anderson, patroness of the Female Orphan Asylum of Petersburg, awarded these silver scholastic medals to outstanding students in 1814. **Virginia Historical Society, photograph by Katherine Wetzel.**

19. Nine-year-old Mary Elizabeth Effinger, of Harrisonburg, completed this silk-on-linen sampler on 30 September—1834. **Collection of Mr. and Mrs. Fred Scott, photograph by Katherine Wetzel.**

20. *Above:* The left panel of this partisan wood engraving published in New York on 23 May 1863 in *Leslie's Illustrated Newspaper* depicted "Southern women hounding their men on to rebellion," while the right panel showed them "feeling the effects of rebellion, and creating bread riots." Virginia State Library. 21. *Below:* Farm women in Virginia were no strangers to the plow. Virginia State Library, gift of M. G. Goodpasture, Ferrum College, Ferrum, Virginia.

22. Cigarette manufacturers in post–Civil War Virginia employed scores of women, black and white, in their factories. **Virginia State Library.**

23. Virginia belles were among the women whose faces inspired Charles Dana Gibson to create idealized images of the Gibson girl *(below left)* in drawings such as *A Daughter of the South* (New York, ca. 1909). **Library of Congress.** 24. Industrialism took sewing out of the home and into the factory. This early twentieth-century photograph *(below right)* shows Katie Wimer working as a seamer in a hosiery mill in Staunton, Virginia. **Virginia State Library.**

25. A twentieth-century photograph records a cascade of partially assembled shoes created by women working at the Craddock-Terry factory in Lynchburg *(above)*. **Virginia State Library.** 26. Woman suffrage advocates *(below)* photographed in Capitol Square, Richmond, after a "Votes for Women" rally. Adèle Clark is standing at the left, and Nora Houston is seated *(third from left)* in the automobile. **Virginia Historical Society.**

27. *Above:* This card advertising a speech by Lila Meade Valentine is preserved at the Virginia State Library. 28. *Below left:* Richmond entrepreneur Ellen Tompkins Kidd founded her Pin Money Pickle company in the 1870s, and when she retired in 1927 her company was grossing half a million dollars annually. **Collection of James K. Taylor, photograph by Katherine Wetzel. 29.** *Below right:* Norfolk's Sarah Lee Fain, one of the first two women in the General Assembly, became in 1930 the first Virginia woman to run for Congress—the occasion of this cartoon by Fred O. Seibel. **Special Collections—Virginia Commonwealth University, photograph by Katherine Wetzel.**

30. During and after the Great Depression, photographers recorded life in the Blue Ridge Mountains *(above left)* even as legions of federally employed laborers were building Shenandoah National Park and the Skyline Drive. **Virginia State Library. 31.** Lucy Randolph Mason in 1937 *(above right).* Mason became head of the National Consumers League in 1932 and later was a southern union organizer for the Congress of Industrial Organizations. **Southern Historical Collection, University of North Carolina—Chapel Hill, photograph by Katherine Wetzel. 32.** Eleanor Roosevelt *(below)* visiting the White Top Folk Festival, an annual festival founded in 1931 by Virginia composer Annabel Morris Buchanan, of Marion. **Virginia State Library.**

small farms suffered terribly from the shortage of manpower, as they owned no slaves and their men were too poor to buy their way out of the army. One such woman wrote her husband that if he did not come home soon, " 'Twant be no use to come, for we'll . . . be out there . . . in the old grave yard with your ma and pa."[21] And many a woman who had been accustomed to wealth knew by 1864 what it was to be hungry, homeless, and desperate for food for her children.

All the while, there was the relentless killing. Lucy Breckinridge, of Botetourt, attended a gathering on a neighboring plantation late in 1862. Fourteen women were there, and every one was in deep mourning. Many women did not even know the fate of their men. Mary Boykin Chestnut described a mother's search for her son among soldiers who had just been returned from a Northern prison. "She was utterly unconscious of the crowd. The anxious dread—expectation—hurry and hope which led her on showed in her face." The woman did not find her son, but not for lack of trying. "She kept going in and out among them, with a basket of provisions she had brought for him to eat. It was too pitiful."[22]

The Confederacy finally submitted in April 1865. Although signs of defeat had been everywhere, many white women were nonetheless shocked and deeply depressed. "I feel as if there was nothing more to live for in this world," Emma Mordecai told her diary.[23] Many other diaries, begun in the first flush of the war, simply came to a dead stop.

Only a few miles from the scene of the surrender at Appomattox Court House, Fanny Berry learned that she was indeed free. "Never was no time like 'em befo' or since," she recalled. "Niggers shoutin' an' clappin' hands an' singin'! Chillun runnin' all over de place beatin' tins and yellin'. . . . Sho' did some celebratin'. "[24] When the Confederacy collapsed, chattel slavery collapsed with it. This was a signally important event, and it takes first place as we assess the impact of war on Virginia women. But we could also wish that slavery had been ended some other way. The war was unspeakably destructive. Many of the major battles were fought on Virginia soil, and some areas were contested again and again. Winchester changed hands so many times (seventy or more) that no one could keep an exact count. By the war's end factories were shut down, railroads and bridges were destroyed, and a large part of Richmond was in ashes. Just about everyone was poor.

None of this boded well for women. In the emergencies of war, women had discovered in themselves new reserves of competence and courage. The question is: How much did this gain them after the war was over? Pending further research, for white women the war appears to have been ultimately a setback. And for black women the uphill struggle for genuine freedom was made even steeper by the poverty of war-torn Virginia.

Black women took up the challenge with a will, though, and in the drive for education they achieved a great deal. In the new Constitution of 1869 Virginia at last provided for a tax-supported public school system, and gradually a network of racially segregated elementary schools came into being. Greater numbers of students meant a greater demand for teachers, and lobbying efforts by black parents increasingly resulted in decisions to hire black teachers in black schools. In 1882 the General Assembly contributed to the training of those teachers by establishing the Virginia Normal and Collegiate Institute (now Virginia State University), the first fully state-supported black college in the United States.

The state left much undone, however, and only by sacrifice and imagination did black communities provide high-quality education for their children. School districts ordinarily supplied a building, a salary for the teacher, and precious little else. Virginia Estelle Randolph was only eighteen when she accepted her first teaching assignment at Mountain Road School in Henrico. She arrived to find a small building on a bare clay hill, and she decided that among her many projects she would dignify her school by improving the grounds. She mobilized the neighborhood; they leveled the ground, hauled in topsoil, planted grass, and, finally, planted twelve trees, which they named after the twelve disciples. Judas, alas, had to be cut down a few years later when Randolph's continuing success resulted in the expansion of the building.[25]

Virginia Randolph was representative of a corps of young black teachers who saw themselves as missionaries. To them education was the key to the progress of black people, and to this cause they brought the energy of true believers. Rosa Dixon Bowser, one of Richmond's first black public school teachers, organized a night school for men and boys, and, since teaching day and night still left the weekends open, she spent the seventh day teaching Sunday school. So did Virginia Randolph. So did Lucy F. Simms, who taught three generations of black children in Harrisonburg. Born a slave in 1855 Simms graduated from Hampton Institute in 1874. She maintained close ties with her alma mater. One of her letters still survives, a letter asking Hampton's president to admit one of her most promising students. "She would like dress-making or millinery," Simms explained, "but her parents are not able to send her off to learn them. She cuts, fits and makes most of the family's clothes now. Is there a chance for such a girl to get in there and work her way thru school?"[26]

Most school districts provided no schooling for blacks beyond the elementary grades, and this, as Lucy Simms's request suggests, presented a crisis for students who wanted to go on. For many students there was no solution. For some, however, there was the "industrial" school. Hampton was the most famous of these, and while the school received some money from northern white contributors (it was also run by whites in the early decades), it could not have survived without the labor of its students, all of whom were blacks or Indians, half of them female. Students worked in kitchens, in the laundry, in shops, in the sawmill, or on the farm. A select group known as the Hampton Singers went on concert tours. They raised thousands of dollars and "sang up" Virginia Hall, the women's dormitory.[27]

By 1900 there were more than thirty private schools for blacks in Virginia, about half of them founded and controlled by blacks and about half by whites. The most remarkable founder of them all was Jennie Dean. Born a slave and raised on a farm in Prince William County, Jennie Dean went to work as a domestic in Washington, D.C., saving her wages to pay the mortgage on the family farm and to send her younger sister to school. She soon proved to be a superb organizer. In the summers she returned home, where she first organized a Sunday school, then a church. She began teaching Saturday classes in cooking and sewing, and before long she began to believe she could build a school.

She went to Massachusetts in 1891, signed on as a boarding-house cook, and began making her case to anyone who would listen. In 1893 she appealed to Susan B. Anthony to let her speak to the National Woman Suffrage Association Convention in Washington. Anthony bent the rules, Dean made the speech, and a pledge of $2,000 was the result. The Manassas Industrial School for the Training of Colored Youth opened soon thereafter.[28]

Jennie Dean continued as the school's guiding spirit and chief fund raiser. While the largest sums came from northern donors, Dean did what she had done since her Sunday school days: She urged even the poorest of her neighbors to contribute what they could—farm produce, livestock, or a day's labor, if not cash—and their contributions, sometimes as little as a nickel's worth, were faithfully recorded, right along with those of the Rockefellers and Carnegies.[29]

The students contributed, too. The Manassas School, even more than Hampton, emphasized manual labor; the students spent half of each day at their books and half at trades. "Our school is not intended to make ladies and gentlemen," Dean was quoted as saying, "but useful, honest farmers and house servants. . . . If Providence intended them to do something else, they will be called to their appointed task in due time."[30]

This approach had its critics, many of them black, who did not think that ambitious students should have to wait around for Providence and who feared that industrial schools encouraged their students to settle for menial occupations. To the extent that black schools depended on white money, however, their promoters, whatever their personal and private opinions, had little choice but to sing the praises of manual labor in their public statements. And if they needed proof, they had only to look at the action of the General Assembly in 1902. Since its founding in 1882, the Virginia Normal and Collegiate Institute had stood for the right of black students to aim high—to earn regular degrees and to aspire to postgraduate and professional training. In 1902 the legislature revoked the power of VNCI to grant bachelor's degrees; they substituted industrial for academic education; and they changed the name to the Virginia Normal and Industrial Institute.[31]

This was not an isolated incident. Instead, it was one step in the South's march toward increasing racial discrimination, discrimination that was systematic, overt, and increasingly written into law. Virginia had already taken a giant step in that direction with the Constitution of 1902, which through a poll tax and other devices took the vote away from more than nine-tenths of black men. Blacks were excluded by custom from patronizing most hotels, theaters, and restaurants, and where custom was insufficient, the law was brought to bear. After decades in which blacks and whites had been riding on the same streetcars and railroad cars, the General Assembly in 1900 and 1906 required transportation companies to provide separate cars. As though this was not enough, there was also sporadic terrorism. During the 1890s an average of four or five blacks were lynched in Virginia each year.[32]

Given the context of growing repression and fear, the achievements of black educators stand out all the more vividly. There was also pervasive poverty, of course, and that was a decisive factor as black and white women worked out their own race relations, one-on-one, in kitchens all over Virginia.

The transition out of slavery was not easy for anyone, and in many instances the immediate result was alienation between white women and their former slaves. When slavery was ended, large numbers of ex-slaves exercised their newfound liberty by leaving, and the house servants—whose nearness to their

owners had intensified the psychological burdens of slavery—
were often the first to go. As one former owner put it, "Those
we loved best, and who loved us best—as we thought—were the
first to leave us." This was a bitter pill to take for white women
who saw themselves as having continually sacrificed for their
slaves' welfare; their own self-esteem depended on the slaves'
standing fast and expressing gratitude. When the former slaves
followed their own agendas—searching for relatives or for new
work, or just finding out what it was like to come and go at
will—their former owners were confused and hostile.[33]

From the ex-slaves' point of view, they themselves had been
sacrificing since they were old enough to work, and the former
owners were the ones guilty of ingratitude, expecting their
former slaves to work for next to nothing. The records of the
Freedmen's Bureau, a federal agency charged with supervising
the transition to free labor, were filled with complaints from
blacks accusing their employers of breach of contract. In the
case of "Martha, a freedman vs. Sterling Cooke," for example,
the bureau ruled "that said Cooke is to furnish said woman
Martha with sufficient cotton and wool for her winter clothing.
The said Martha to spin it and said Cooke to have it woven.
Also said Cooke to give said Martha two barrels of corn."[34]

These were small amounts—in goods, not cash—and they
point up the problems of Virginia's postwar economy: Some
whites could provide land; most blacks and poorer whites could
provide labor; but no one had much cash or credit. One
consequence was that many black women took jobs in domestic
service, working extremely long hours for extremely low wages.
Another was that many thousands of families, both black and
white, became renters or sharecroppers, making the barest of
livings and accumulating inescapable debts to landlords and
storekeepers. That so many of them eventually acquired small
plots of their own was a tribute to their persistence. In Louisa
County in 1870 only 2 percent of the landowners were black.
By 1900, 39 percent were black, and whites, too, had made
progress in moving from sharecropping to owning some small
patch of ground.[35]

While Virginia's postwar poverty strained relationships between the employer and the employed, it also called forth
creative experiments in mutual aid. In Norfolk in 1867 a group
of black women founded a life insurance organization called the
United Order of Tents. Run entirely by women, the Tents paid
benefits to the heirs of many thousands of members over the
years. Some enterprising white women, meanwhile, took up the
cause of the "gentlewoman" in distress. In Charlottesville,
Lynchburg, Norfolk, Richmond, and Staunton, they established exchanges for women's work, stores that sold needlework,
handicrafts, preserves, and bakery goods on consignment. And
in a dozen Virginia cities, working women, both white and
black, formed "women's assemblies" of the Knights of Labor, a
short-lived but farsighted labor union.[36]

Unfortunately, none of these groups was able to change the
fundamentally wretched position of women in the labor force
(although the Knights of Labor, had they lasted longer, would
surely have tried). As was true the country over, women in
postwar Virginia were concentrated in occupations of low pay,
low prestige, long hours, poor conditions, with no chance of
advancement. While this had been true for a long time, by the
end of the nineteenth century the United States census office
was keeping detailed statistics that made women's occupational
status painfully clear. In 1900 more than 125,000 Virginia
women were gainfully employed. Only 6 percent of them were
professionals, almost all of them teachers. Another 3 percent
were salaried employees, mainly saleswomen and secretaries,
and 10 percent were farmers (usually widows). The majority, 58
percent, were domestic servants, laundresses, and waitresses.
Adding in agricultural laborers (8 percent), factory hands (5
percent), and seamstresses (6.5 percent), a full three-quarters of
Virginia's women workers had jobs at the bottom of the occupational ladder.[37]

A job at the bottom meant, among other things, low wages—
much lower than men's, even for comparable work. In 1890
female hands in tobacco factories were paid on the average $120
a year. Men were paid $238. In the cotton mills the women

averaged $151, while the men took home $304. Even the men's wages were not enough to support a family, so most families scraped through by putting teen-aged children to work. Some of the workers in the cotton mills were as young as seven or eight.[38]

Millhands worked whatever hours the managers decided upon. When they were laid off—sometimes for weeks or even months at a stretch—there were no unemployment benefits. If they were injured on the job, there was no disability pay. When employers wanted to speed up production, then employees worked very long hours. Anthelia Holt, a farmer's daughter from Matoaca, wrote a friend that she was working in the mill until after seven every night and until four on Saturdays, "so you may know that I am in the penitentiary now for we wont see any thing out doors only on Sunday."[39]

Anthelia Holt was a spirited young woman though, and, in her letters to her friend Lottie Clark, she shook off the deadening routine of the cotton mill by concentrating on other things. She wrote about church, holidays, weddings, and her desire to go to school. At times, she wrote with humor; she had her picture taken and promised to send one "to keep the hawks away from your grand Mars chickins." Like most nineteenth-century correspondents, she wrote a great deal about health. "This leaves all up but not well" was a common refrain. And like many other nineteenth-century women, she was perfectly open in her loving feelings for her friend: "I wish you were here to sleep with me"; "write soon write soon my dear little darling."[40]

All the while, "your ever loveing friend Anthelia Holt" kept Lottie informed of her "mashes." A mash was a boyfriend or potential boyfriend. To "make a mash" was to catch the eye of a young man. To "be mashed" was to be lovestruck. Anthelia triumphed on an April evening in 1889, when she "made several mashes five young men wonted to take me to church Sunday night I hardly knew what to do."[41]

Whether Anthelia Holt made her final mash and got married is not known. If she did, she probably quit the mill. Married women typically did not stay in the paid labor force unless their husbands were disabled, unemployed, or very poor. This was in part a matter of social pressure. But it was also a calculated decision. Keeping a home and family going was still enough to tax the strength of any two women. A few laborsaving devices— most notably the sewing machine—were invented before 1900, but the time thus saved was probably taken up with cleaning. The seventeenth and eighteenth centuries had taken little stock in cleanliness, personal or household. But standards went up in the nineteenth century, and so, accordingly, did the demands on the housewife.

In most household tasks women still started from scratch. For example, an 1889 cookbook (the *Housekeeper's Companion* by Bessie Gunter, of Accomack) gave a recipe for turtle: "Before cooking a terrapin allow it to swim about for three or four hours in cold water." On farms—and 85 percent of Virginians were still farmers—women not only ran household operations but were also called into the fields during the busiest seasons. A Chesterfield County farmer in 1878 recorded the labors of his wife during spring planting: "Wife & children planted 1/2 acre in corn"; "wife & children planted the corn and put guano in hill"; "wife & children helped to pick grass out of tobacco plant bed by gate."[42] Meantime, there were all the tasks of child rearing. The typical woman in postwar Virginia, whether white or black, bore five or six children.[43]

For most married women, staying home made good economic sense. Running a household was more than a full-time job as it was, and it did offer some opportunities to make money. Many thousands of Virginia women took in sewing or washing, looked after boarders or lodgers, made wine or corn liquor, or sent milk, eggs, or garden produce to market. Even city women did this. As late as 1900 it was still possible to raise cows, hogs, or chickens in towns. In any case, the average married women had no cause to go looking for a job. Even if she found one, the work was likely to be oppressive and the earnings so little that once she figured in child care and other costs, the job would simply not pay.

When it was possible and when it paid, Virginia women did

seek careers, highly visible careers, and they combined their careers with raising families. The most successful business-women in nineteenth-century Virginia were the milliners and dressmakers, and they generally did not close their shops when they married or when they had children. Instead, they hired help—at home or in the shop as needed—and stayed in business without missing a stitch.[44]

There was not very much room at the top, however. Al-though the Civil War—the poverty, the dislocation, and the killing and crippling of many men—pushed more women than ever before into the labor market, the opportunities available to women did not expand in proportion to women's talents and needs. In the business world there were no noticeable improve-ments. During the war women had demonstrated their worth as clerical workers, but their jobs evaporated with the fall of the Confederacy. There were fewer female clerks in Richmond in 1890 than there had been in 1863.[45]

In the aftermath of war, to be sure, some women engaged in conventionally masculine businesses. Maria Louisa Avery, of Petersburg, for example, ran a large scrap metal concern. (*She* called it scrap metal; the city directory listed her under "junk.") But this only continued a long-standing pattern in which wid-ows took over from their deceased husbands. Before the war such women had appeared among Petersburg's butchers, black-smiths, saddlers, and freight haulers. After the war women's access to careers in business may actually have narrowed, as family businesses became less important relative to corpora-tions. The latter were run by officers and directors, none of whom were likely to be women. As businesses grew bigger, in other words, women were more likely to be excluded from management.[46]

Literature, on the other hand, was a widening field for female talent, and a number of Virginia women achieved national fame for their writing. In the 1820s a revolution in printing produced magazines and books at a price middle-class Americans could afford. Those who purchased books were mainly women, and they provided an enthusiastic market for the work of female authors. Mary Randolph was probably the first Virginia woman writer to taste success in the new market. In 1824 she brought out *The Virginia House-wife*, America's first regional cookbook. By 1850 it had gone through eleven editions.[47]

Mary Virginia Terhune, known to millions as Marion Harland, commenced her writing career with the novel *Alone* in 1854. Over the next sixty-eight years she married, had six children, and wrote twenty-five novels, twenty-five books of household advice, and numerous histories and biographies. Constance Cary Harrison was another prolific author who wrote both novels and advice books, and Amélie Rives made the best-seller list in 1888 with *The Quick or the Dead?* A Virginia woman also produced what may have been the first best-seller by a black American; Elizabeth Keckley, dressmaker and confidante of Mary Todd Lincoln, wrote *Behind the Scenes* in 1868. A devastating exposé of life inside the White House, the book has since become an important source for Lincoln scholars.[48]

In music Virginia's premier professional was Sissieretta Jones. Born in Portsmouth in 1869, Jones began by singing in church, and after her parents moved to Rhode Island she acquired a classical music education. Jones soon was hailed as the Black Patti, a reference to Italian opera star Adelina Patti. Although Jones gave a number of highly prestigious concerts, including a command performance at the White House, racial prejudice precluded her singing with opera companies. As segregation grew more rigid, she was unable to obtain concert engagements for white audiences after 1895. Undaunted, she organized the Black Patti Troubadours. For nineteen seasons this versatile troupe entertained black audiences in Virginia and points north, presenting programs of comedy, art songs, opera, and music from the black gospel and folk traditions. Visual artists had a far more difficult time making a living. Sallie Mahood, a portrait painter from Lynchburg, was one of the few who did. Other notable Virginia women painters included Susan (or Susannah) F. Q. Nicholson and Jane Braddick Peticolas in the antebellum period and Lelia Cocke and Mary DeLeftwich Dodge in the postwar era.[49]

In the professions, prospects were mixed. The educated woman's best chance was schoolteaching, as the expanding public school system opened up unprecedented numbers of new positions. While teaching was the one profession that welcomed large numbers of women, a few bold souls pioneered in new professional endeavors. In the mission field, Virginia's outstanding leader was Lottie Digges Moon, a native of Albemarle County and a Baptist missionary to China for nearly forty years. Lottie Moon was not the first American woman missionary in China. That distinction seems to belong to another Virginian, Henrietta Hall Shuck, who was married in 1835 and set off with her husband only two days later to take the gospel to the people of China. Immensely dedicated but eventually worn down by the cares of the mission and of motherhood, Shuck died at the age of twenty-seven, in childbirth with her fifth child.[50]

Lottie Moon sailed for China in 1873, one of a new generation of single women missionaries. Out in the field, these women accomplished things they could never have begun at home—Lottie Moon founded her own church—and they resented it when their superiors tried to check them. In 1885 the Foreign Mission Board announced that women missionaries would not be allowed to vote in mission meetings. Moon resigned in protest, and the board quickly revoked its ruling. Moon was also a staunch and effective advocate of the right of women back home to organize in support of the mission movement. The Woman's Missionary Union of the Southern Baptist Convention was founded in 1888, largely as a result of her efforts. Lottie Moon went on to become the patron saint of Southern Baptist missions. When famine came to her region in 1912, she spent most of her salary to feed others. She herself was laid low by malnutrition. She died en route to the United States at the age of seventy-two.[51]

Lottie Moon came from a remarkable family. In 1857 her older sister, Orianna Russell Moon, was graduated from the Female Medical College of Pennsylvania—apparently the first southern woman to earn a medical degree. (The first American woman to do so was Elizabeth Blackwell in 1849.) Dr. Moon went on to marry another physician whom she met while serving in a Confederate hospital in Charlottesville, and afterwards she practiced in association with him.[52]

Rebecca Lee, meanwhile, was preparing to score another medical first. Born in Richmond in 1833, Rebecca Lee was graduated from the New England Woman's Medical College in 1864, becoming the first American-born black woman to earn a medical degree. When the war was over, Dr. Lee returned to Richmond, where she conducted a successful practice.[53]

Still another first was registered by Emily Chenault Runyon, the first women to be admitted to the Richmond Academy of Medicine and to the Virginia Medical Society and thus the first to receive full professional recognition from the male medical establishment. Dr. Runyon, born in Kentucky and educated in the Midwest, arrived in Richmond in 1895, a young widow with two small children. She was soon in the news. When a colleague proposed her for admission to the Richmond Academy of Medicine, other members threatened to bolt the organization. One of them, W. W. Parker, was already famous for his harangues against professional women. "We hear of . . . woman's rights," he wrote, "better and wiser than 'Moses and the prophets'; the anti-poverty party, women lawyers and doctors, maligning the old family doctor—miscegenation, free love. The woman sheriff and mayor, leading *inevitably* to the woman *voter*, member of Congress, judge, and finally petticoat President of the United States." To allow women to practice medicine or law, Parker went on, "aims at the complete destruction of society, subversion of religion, and reign of chaos."[54]

Parker's attacks were so venomous that they boomeranged, winning new supporters for the women doctors' side. In any event, Emily Chenault Runyon was admitted to the local and state medical societies and went on to build a large practice. Parker was not to be entirely dismissed, however. When he connected the licensing of a handful of female professionals to the "reign of chaos," he was only restating a classic tenet of the cult of true womanhood: When woman steps out of her sphere, the entire social order is in jeopardy. This belief was still powerful in Virginia. At the same time, it could be (and was) argued that women physicians would actually foster true womanhood: Women doctors helped preserve feminine delicacy by giving female patients an alternative to examinations by men. Indeed, most of the early female physicians treated women and children only.

With the practice of law, however, the legislature drew the line. In 1892 the General Assembly passed an act stating that "any person" who met certain requirements could be licensed to practice law. Two years later Belva Lockwood, a Washington attorney, applied for permission to practice in Virginia. One court denied her, but she initiated a successful appeal, and thus became the first woman lawyer licensed in Virginia. Had that been the end of the story, it would have been a happy ending. But the legislature wrote the last chapter. When they next convened in 1895–1896, Virginia's lawmakers changed "any person" to "any male citizen" and with that change of phrase took away the right of Virginia women to practice law.[55]

Legal conservatism was of course not new in Virginia. In 1877 when Virginia finally granted married women the right to own property in their own names, it was the last state in the United States to do so.[56] This raises the question of how well Virginia women fared relative to women in other parts of the country. No systematic research has yet been done on this question, but preliminary evidence suggests that Virginia women and southern women generally did not do very well.

As early as the 1820s Virginians who visited northern cities were struck by the greater independence of the women there. Eliza Ruffin was fascinated with Philadelphia. Women drove carriages; they walked the streets alone day and night ("no wonder their feet are so large and spraddling"); and above all they did a great deal of business: "entered a Shoe-Store, business carried on in a large scale and managed entirely by the females who not merely *sew* them but *sale* them too with their delicate hands not a male to be seen behind many counters."[57] Thirty years later Mary Blackford visited Philadelphia, and she, too, was impressed by women walking out at night and by the number of occupations open to them. "You see them in all the stores and shops, and women go out white washing, and in many ways get a comfortable support that are not opened to our poor." Then she added, "I wish Va was not so well satisfied with herself, and did not despise the North so much, she might learn so much from them."[58]

The war probably widened the gap. The North emerged from the war self-confident and economically vigorous. Women did not make progress on all fronts; in 1873, for example, the Comstock law lumped contraception together with pornography, making it a crime to mail contraceptive devices or information or to transport them across state lines. Nonetheless, a burgeoning woman's rights movement achieved some important gains. Women got the vote in Wyoming Territory in 1869. By 1890 women in nineteen states were voting in school elections, and by 1896 the women of four western states voted on equal terms with men. It was an important time, moreover, for higher education. In the postwar era several of the best universities opened their doors to women—for undergraduate, graduate, and professional training—and a number of distinguished women's colleges were founded as well.[59]

Virginia, on the other hand, emerged from the war with a devastated economy. Among whites there was a pervasive feeling of defeat and a menacing sense that their world had been turned upside down. The once rich, after all, were now poor; the slaves were free; and some of the former slaves were even voting and holding office. These conditions did not encourage experimentation. In the immediate aftermath of the war, the pressure on women to follow conventional paths probably intensified.

In any case, no woman's rights movement took hold in Virginia until the twentieth century. Nor did educational opportunities keep pace with those in the North. As late as 1905 a confidential report on higher education in Virginia named Randolph-Macon Woman's College as the one women's college deserving of high marks for academic excellence. And it was no coincidence that all the women physicians discussed earlier went north for their medical training.[60]

When it came to individual action, only a few highly exceptional people made public expressions of unconventional opinions. Elizabeth Van Lew, the former Union spy, was already a social outcast when she took up the cause of woman suffrage. Every year she paid her taxes under protest, pointing out, as Hannah Lee Corbin had a century earlier, that she was subject to taxation without representation.[61]

Orra Langhorne, who was born in Harrisonburg and spent her married life in Lynchburg and her widowhood in Culpeper, was another maverick—one who managed to stay on speaking terms with family and friends while she pursued her unusually liberal course. Langhorne was a journalist, and she wrote with unfailing (also unfounded) optimism about the rights of women and the rights of black people. Never one to sneeze at new ideas, she enrolled as a special student at Randolph-Macon Woman's College at the age of fifty-six.[62]

Elmina Slenker, of Snowville, in Pulaski County was actually jailed briefly for her ideas. Slenker was a freethinker (a person who believed that religion was a hoax) and a sex radical (someone who believed that sexuality should be openly discussed and reformed), and she published her arguments in the columns of reform journals and in novels such as *The Clergyman's Victims* and *Mary Jones, Infidel School Teacher*. In 1886 a federal agent posing as a fellow reformer sent Slenker a request for more information. She complied, and six months later she was arrested under the Comstock law for sending "obscene, lewd, and lascivious writings" through the United States mail. She was tried in Wytheville, and the jury found her guilty. The judge, however, turned her loose on the grounds that she had not known that her materials were obscene. During her trial the citizens of Snowville had come forward to testify to her good character, and after she came home they continued to tolerate the kindly eccentric in their midst.[63]

Whatever their particular beliefs, these were women who along with the educators and missionaries had their vision fixed on the future. In the wake of war other Virginia women focused on the past. White women in many parts of the state formed memorial societies. They located the remains of Confederate soldiers and had them removed from makeshift graves to new or refurbished cemeteries. They marked the graves, erected monuments, and held annual commemorative services. Had the Confederacy won the war, as one such society explained in 1866, all this would have been carried out with pride by the government of the new nation. As it was, "the melancholy yet grateful task" fell to the women.[64]

Like all organizations in this period, the memorial societies were hobbled by "the extreme poverty of our people." They also struggled with the desire of many men to forget. The Ladies' Memorial Association of Petersburg found the men "seemingly unwilling to assist the ladies. . . . As patriotism and herosim appear to be entirely dead," the women intoned, they would have to proceed on their own. Not until the turn of the century did they encounter widespread enthusiasm for enshrining the Lost Cause.[65]

In the twenty-odd years after the war, the majority of Virginians were too preoccupied with survival in the present to give much attention to either the future or the past. They must have given something special to their daughters, however. A new generation was on the rise, a generation born too late to have suffered the traumas of slavery or of war. As they came of age, Virginia women would burst onto the public scene with an energy that had never been seen before.

5

"Struggle for the Liberation of Personality"

The Modern Era

The twentieth century has received short shrift from Virginia historians. From the standpoint of women this is unfortunate, for the early twentieth century may well have been women's greatest age. The Progressive Era—the period from the late 1890s to the First World War—was a time of reform in all parts of the nation. Some Progressives tried to reform government and the political system; others sought to discipline big business. Still others worked toward a more humane and democratic society, meaning among other things a society that opened more doors to women. In Virginia, as in the rest of the country, this social justice movement within progressivism was largely a women's movement.

The tide turned in the 1920s. For the next forty years, their contributions during both world wars notwithstanding, Virginia women found themselves under pressure to withdraw from public life and to concentrate on homes and families. The pressure was in many respects effective. But family life itself was undergoing dramatic changes, and from 1940 on more and more women entered the paid labor force. Then came the civil rights movement and a revived woman's rights movement was not far behind. All of this prompted a rethinking of the roles of women and men, even among those who did not see themselves as sympathetic to the new feminism; by the 1970s, for the first time ever, significant numbers of Virginians took seriously the idea of equality between the sexes. The consequences are still unfolding.

•

There was a new image for the new age—the Gibson girl, first created by lithographer Charles Dana Gibson in 1890. In 1893 Gibson met Irene Langhorne, a Virginia beauty who more than matched his ideal. "When she came in," her sister later wrote of her, "it was like the sun streaming into the room." Dana Gibson and Irene Langhorne were married in 1895, and she became one of his favorite models. From the middle nineties to the First World War, her image appeared everywhere, "in homes, in college rooms, in rude mining cabins in the Klondike."[1]

Tall, athletic, and radiantly self-possessed, the Gibson girl captured a certain restless and independent spirit among American women. That spirit was manifested, too, in simplified fashions and in a new emphasis on physical fitness. Out went hoops and petticoats; in came the shirtwaist, a tailored blouse modeled after a man's shirt (except that the buttons fastened up the back) and worn with a jacket and skirt. The new look still made the most of a small waist, so the temptations of tight lacing remained. But by the 1890s anyone who wore a confining corset did so in opposition to a chorus of reformers. In 1897 the catalog of Hartshorn Memorial College, a school for black women (now part of Virginia Union University), pleaded with the mothers of students "to throw away the disease-producing corset, and give your girls a chance to breathe and grow—to grow strong and well. *The tight corset*," the catalog insisted, "*is nothing else than the skeleton-angel with his whetted scythe.*"[2]

The colleges were leaders in the campaign for physical exercise. In 1873 a Boston physician had condemned coeducation on the grounds that girls who studied during their menstrual periods would divert energy from their ovaries to their brains, causing the ovaries to shrivel and the girls themselves to become weak, infertile, or even mentally deranged. The theory touched off a national uproar; the women's colleges were on the defensive and felt obliged to prove that higher education and good health were compatible. To that end the colleges championed exercise. "Girls at boarding schools must take much physical exercise," the Hollins Institute catalog warned in 1890, "failing to do this, they wilt and wither and make feeble women." Hollins students were required to come prepared with heavy walking shoes and overshoes for long hikes through the hills. They played tennis, skated, and tobogganed, and in 1897 they chose up sides for basketball, getting their first experience of competitive team sports.[3]

Outside the colleges, too, Virginia women of the sedentary classes were looking for new routes to fitness. Horseback riding, long in vogue among the wealthy, enjoyed renewed popularity among those who could afford it. In 1894, meanwhile, the *Richmond Times* reported a daring innovation—the physical culture class. Three mornings a week, forty-two ladies gathered for calisthenics, gymnastics, and basketball. The reporter tried to describe how the game was played: "Now somebody catches [the ball], and turning away from them all and bending low over it, tries to carry it in little bounces around the edge of the hall to the goal." The reporter also assured readers that the same women who would "rush, tear and scramble" after the ball emerged from the locker room "the most decorous and dignified of womankind."[4]

Such assurances were commonplace as women in all parts of the state launched new organizations and explored new fields of collective endeavor. In 1898 women of Abingdon Presbytery asked permission to form a Woman's Missionary Union. The men of the presbytery voted this idea down. The women then set about quieting the men's anxiety: "We do not wish to usurp any authority or overstep the bounds of womanly propriety," they explained, "but simply, as Presbyterian women, work . . . systematically, unitedly and prayerfully, under the constitution and by-laws drawn up by the committee appointed by Presbytery." The men relented, and the women got their union.[5]

The Woman's Christian Temperance Union, organized on the state level in Virginia in 1883, felt similar pressure to demonstrate its respectability. The state president made her position clear in 1888: "We . . . have nothing whatever to do with the ballot for woman. My own opinion is that its advocacy in this State would lose us many zealous sympathizers, and seriously imperil our usefulness."[6]

At the same time, women without the vote were severely handicapped when it came to influencing the General Assembly. In the legislative session of 1887–1888, the WCTU asked for two new laws, one to require "Scientific Temperance Instruction" in the public schools and the other to toughen the state's statutory rape provisions.[7] The legislature took neither bill seriously. Failure, however, was an eye-opening experience. After the statutory rape bill failed a second time, a WCTU spokeswoman called for the licensing of "lawyers of our own sex who will take time and trouble to study the laws for women, and aid in making such as will elevate and not degrade." And just two years later, in 1892, the annual convention of the Virginia WCTU issued a rousing feminist resolution: "That we sympathize with, and will aid by all right means, in any movement that looks to the enlargement of woman's sphere of usefulness and her elevation and advancement in life."[8]

The WCTU did score one legislative victory in its early years, a law providing that a matron, not a male warden, should be in charge of female prisoners in the state penitentiary. But this was only one victory in a sea of losses, and the conclusion was inescapable: Politicians were not on the whole responsive to women's concerns. If the WCTU wanted proper laws for children, for women, and for protection of the home, the women themselves would have to take a much larger part in the world.[9]

But exactly what roles would women be allowed to play? The answer to that question became apparent only gradually, as one new organization after another defined its goals and went to work. Some met with instant success, others with stiff resistance. Together, they steadily expanded women's sphere, until by 1915 they had achieved nothing less than an organizational revolution in Virginia.

Among the first of the causes taken up by Virginia women was the preservation of historic sites. For this there was an important precedent; the first preservation organization run by American women was the Mount Vernon Ladies' Association of the Union, chartered in 1856. The rescue of Mount Vernon was the brainchild of South Carolinian Ann Pamela Cunningham, who was sometimes an invalid, always iron-willed, and often controversial. Under her determined leadership, the association purchased the property, survived the war, and began the painstaking process of restoration. Cunningham was eased out in 1873, but the association forged ahead, continuing to develop the site until it at last looked like the national treasure that it is.[10]

Virginia was full of historic treasures, and by the late nineteenth century many of them were in advanced stages of decay. In 1889 a small group of women who for years had watched the weeds overgrow Williamsburg gathered to form the Association for the Preservation of Virginia Antiquities. They weeded and raked in Williamsburg and Jamestown, hauled bricks, raised money, and began to acquire title to sites. Before long the forces of preservation were strengthened by the rise of hereditary patriotic societies. The Daughters of the American Revolution, the Virginia Society of Colonial Dames, and the United Daughters of the Confederacy all were founded in the 1890s. Among them—and often working in cooperation with one another—these organizations saved countless historic documents, objects, buildings, and sites.[11]

The passion for preserving the materials of Virginia history was part of a larger, indeed a national, women's movement—the woman's club movement. Only a tiny fraction of Virginia women were college educated, but those with some leisure and a little education wanted some way to participate in the literary culture of their time—to read, to discuss, to broaden horizons. Most often the woman's club provided the way. The Progressive

Literary Association, organized by Jewish women in Richmond in 1888, was one of the first in Virginia, and in the next two decades clubs were gathered in almost every community.[12]

The majority of the clubs organized by white women were resolutely literary and at first brooked no discussion of politics. When Mary-Cooke Branch Munford tried to inject a political topic into the proceedings of the Woman's Club of Richmond, the members silenced her by thumping their umbrellas on the floor. As time went on, however, and social reform became a leading concern of American intellectuals, a number of women's clubs took up political issues—for both study and action. Some of the younger clubs were reform minded from the beginning. Such was the Radford Woman's Civic Club, founded in 1912 by women who had discovered an impoverished family living in an abandoned house. The women's clubs also assumed a more activist stance when they joined forces in Lynchburg in 1907 to form the Virginia Federation of Women's Clubs. The new federation resolved to improve education, especially for girls, and instituted a study of the laws affecting women, children, and the educational system.[13]

The clubs formed by black women were often committed to social action from the start. The Richmond Mothers' Club was organized in 1895, and its first project was to raise almost seven hundred dollars for the legal defense of women in Lunenburg County who had been charged with murder. After the women were acquitted, mothers' clubs, expanding under the leadership of the ever-energetic Rosa Dixon Bowser, turned to projects for personal and civic improvement. In 1908 Virginia's black women from various groups came together in Hampton to form the Virginia State Federation of Colored Women's Clubs.[14]

The moving force behind the federation was Janie Porter Barrett. When she assumed the presidency of the Virginia federation in 1908, Barrett was forty-three, married, the mother of four, and already a proven innovator in social service institutions. Shortly after her marriage, she had begun inviting neighborhood girls into her Hampton home for weekly meetings; soon their activities grew into the Locust Street Social Settlement, the first settlement house in Virginia and one of the first in the country for blacks. People came to Locust Street to learn and to do all kinds of particular things, from playing football to quilting to raising chickens, and it was through these activities that the general purposes of the settlement were served—"to get together," as Barrett phrased it, "and discuss the many problems that confront us" in order to improve the life of the community.[15]

The Federation of Colored Women's Clubs, meanwhile, wanted to concentrate its efforts on one major project. Barrett, who once found a nine-year-old girl in the Hampton jail, suggested a home and school for girls in trouble with the law. The federation raised money, bought a farm at Peake's Turnout in Hanover County, and in 1915 opened the Industrial Home School for Colored Girls.

The home school—later renamed the Janie Porter Barrett School—eventually became a model institution, well known and widely imitated. In the beginning, however, it was little more than a worn-out farm surrounded by fearful, angry neighbors. Barrett, whose husband had recently died, moved to the farm herself to win the neighbors over and stayed on as superintendent for more than twenty years.

Donations from private sources and appropriations from the legislature broadened the school's base of support, but the spirit of the school remained Janie Porter Barrett's own. In 1919 she described a discipline measure called the "silent walk." "A silent walk, taking one step and waiting for me to count to five *very* slowly before taking another step, is an excellent remedy for not moving promptly when spoken to." Barrett stood ready to take any student on such a walk at any time of the day or night, and once, when the girls were rowdy in study hall, she took her entire school of sixty-three girls on a silent walk in the dark. It was the kind of discipline—loving, consistent, and attentive in an unfailing personal way—that required as much of the superintendent as it did of the girl. Janie Porter Barrett apparently never begrudged it. "They need much," she wrote of her girls, "because they have had so little."[16]

Coincidentally, the other major figure in rebuilding the lives of girls in trouble was also a Barrett. Kate Waller Barrett, who was white and originally from Stafford County, had her awakening on a proverbial dark and stormy night in the 1890s. Barrett's husband was a clergyman, his parish was the Richmond slum called Butchertown, and it was there that a bedraggled young mother appeared one night, seeking shelter for herself and her baby. The Barretts took her in, and Kate Barrett found her life's work. "It was all so different from what I had thought and imagined," she remembered. "Where was the terrible degradation, the hopeless depravity . . . which I had always been taught to associate with the fallen woman?"[17]

Barrett worked out a new approach to outcast women as she raised her six children, earned a medical degree, and followed her husband to pastorates in Kentucky, Atlanta, and finally Alexandria, Virginia. First, she believed the child should not be punished for the actions of its parents. "There is no such thing as an 'illegitimate child,' " she wrote. Second, mother and child both benefited from staying together. And third, the mothers needed job skills and a chance to be reintegrated into respectable society.[18]

Getting this level-headed message across to the public was not easy. In 1893 Barrett founded a home for unmarried mothers in Atlanta; the protests of neighbors forced her to move the home four times before she finally acquired the backing of the city council. In the meantime she had made contact with Charles N. Crittenton, a millionaire who as a memorial to his daughter devoted himself to the rescue of "fallen" women. In 1896 Kate Waller Barrett, by this time a widow and living in Alexandria, became general superintendent of the Florence Crittenton National Mission, a movement that already counted more than fifty homes for unwed mothers all over the country. This gave Barrett national visibility, and in a reform-minded era she soon became a celebrity, lending both prestige and executive talent to numerous causes. When she died in 1925, the flag over the Capitol in Richmond flew at half-staff; she was believed to be the first woman so honored.[19]

While Kate Waller Barrett was developing programs for the "fallen" woman, a number of others turned their attention to the working woman. The Young Women's Christian Association was their organization, a bridge between wage-earning women and women of the privileged classes. The first YWCA in the South was founded for white women in Richmond in 1887. Women leaders in the black community, too, were anxious to help the working girl, and in 1912 they formed the Phyllis Wheatley Branch, one of the first black YWCAs in the country.

YWCA projects often had small beginnings; when the women of Richmond's Phyllis Wheatley Branch opened their first boardinghouse, they began with a contribution of "one-half-dozen spoons, one quilt, a blanket, two flat irons, one box of Dutch cleanser and two bars of Octagon soap."[20] Programs expanded rapidly, however, and wherever the YWCA appeared in urban Virginia, working women gained access to a range of new services and experiences.

Of special concern was the country girl who arrived in the city, perhaps for the first time in her life, looking for work. YWCA staff met the trains to prevent those young women from falling into the hands of pimps, or as it was phrased at that time, "entering into a life of evil." In 1909 a member of the Richmond YWCA staff reported that she was meeting fifteen trains a day. This was thought to be the origin of the Travelers Aid Society in Virginia. Once taken in hand by the YWCA, the newcomer would have a place to stay, an employment referral service, an invitation to a variety of classes and clubs, and the use of a library and athletic facilities. Working mothers could bring their children to YWCA day-care centers and kindergartens. The YWCA, moreover, did the most to raise public consciousness about the plight of wage-earning women, agitating for protective legislation and opening discussion on the very controversial subject of labor unions. "Sometimes we got into pretty hot water," as Lucy Randolph Mason recalled, "but somehow, we always managed to swim out."[21]

The effectiveness of organized Virginia womanhood was meanwhile becoming apparent on still another front, in the field of public health. Women's groups established hospitals for the poor in Alexandria, Danville, and Richmond. They also pioneered in the care of poor patients outside of the hospitals, and they initiated programs to prevent people from getting sick in the first place.[22]

The foot soldiers in the public health war were professionally trained nurses who not only visited the sick poor in their homes, but also carried with them the gospel of good nutrition, modern prenatal and infant care, soap, sanitation and ventilation, and screens to shut out mosquitoes and flies. In Norfolk the King's Daughters brought the first visiting nurse to Virginia in 1897, and she made the cause more visible by making her rounds on a bicycle. The movement was made stronger in 1902, when the Instructive Visiting Nurses' Association was organized in Richmond.[23]

The inspiration for the IVNA came from Sadie Heath Cabaniss, a Dinwiddie County native who was brought to Richmond in 1894 to take charge of Virginia's first diploma-granting training program for nurses. Sadie Cabaniss awed her trainees; they called her "an angel" and "a born commanding officer" all at once. Certainly her dedication and idealism fired their own, and in 1900 several graduates of her program left the hospital to minister to the poor. Following the example of Lillian Wald in New York, they moved into a house they called the Nurses' Settlement. "At the beginning," one of them reminisced, "when there was nothing in the house save a roll of carpet some one had given us, our great joy was to go over to the house with Miss Cabaniss when we came off duty, sit in a row on the carpet and dream dreams of what we would accomplish."[24]

The IVNA accomplished plenty. The nurses taught classes and staffed the city's home for the aged. They opened Richmond's first tuberculosis dispensary and organized Virginia's first concerted campaign against that prevalent, wasting disease. Beginning in 1913 they added black nurses to their ranks. The IVNA sponsored the city's first juvenile probation officer and helped establish a home for poor working women. It placed nurses in factories and launched visiting nurse programs in Leesburg, Danville, and Newport News. Above all, the nurses made thousands of home visits—"we went into places that even the policemen were aghast" at—affirming daily their commitment to quality health care for everyone.[25]

The organization could not have done so much without the support of community leaders, and here the key figure was Richmond reformer Lila Meade Valentine, the IVNA's founder and for a time its president. For Lila Meade Valentine, as for many others who caught the early twentieth century's spirit of change, one reform led to another. Valentine's concern with public health had been aroused by the sickly children she observed while trying to upgrade the public schools; indeed, she and her friend Mary-Cooke Branch Munford were the dynamic duo of educational reform in Virginia.

They had their work cut out for them. At the turn of the century most of the schools in Virginia were one-room schools. Many of them offered only *very* elementary instruction; Kate Coles of rural Albemarle County, a black woman who had never been to school herself, put it matter-of-factly in 1914: "We have a girl sent to us for teacher she only teaches to the foarth grad same as all of the cuntry schools." The school year averaged six months. Attendance was not compulsory, and on an average day only 30 percent of the eligible pupils actually appeared. Teacher preparation was abysmal. A 1912 survey revealed that 80 percent of Virginia's teachers had no training beyond high school, and a third of the teachers had only an elementary education themselves.[26]

In 1900 Lila Meade Valentine founded the Richmond Educational Association, a citizens' action group dedicated to the betterment of the city schools. Mary-Cooke Branch Munford succeeded Valentine as president of the organization in 1904, and both were instrumental in the success of the Cooperative Education Association, an alliance of women and men who hoped to plant ambitions for better education all over Virginia. Munford raised the money for the famous "May Campaign" of 1905, a campaign in which proschool public speakers blanketed the state. Fifty local leagues, most of them headed by women, were established as a result. And all fifty were soon at work on the formidable problems of Virginia's public schools.[27]

All the while, Mary Munford was preparing for the central crusade of her distinguished reform career, the struggle for a coordinate college for women at the University of Virginia in Charlottesville. For a young white woman of the genteel classes, going to college was an unconventional act, and it took very special circumstances to get her there. Orie Latham Hatcher, later the prime mover in the effort to create new career opportunities for southern women, got her chance when a friend of the family, a northerner, offered to send her to Vassar. This prompted yet another friend of the family (a Virginian) to sputter that he'd see his daughter in hell before he'd send her to a Yankee college. "Well," Orie's father replied, "you see yours in Hell, mine's going to Vassar."[28]

Although Mary Munford had begged her mother to let her go to college, her mother never agreed. Gravely disappointed, Mary Munford channeled her own passion for learning into a passion for seeing that others might learn. In 1910 when she founded the Coordinate College League, the state of Virginia supported four degree-granting colleges for men, but there none for women. There were four normal schools for women, one founded in 1884 in Farmville and others established more recently in Harrisonburg, Fredericksburg, and Radford (respectively the forerunners of Longwood College, James Madison University, Mary Washington College, and Radford University). None gave regular diplomas, however, and none was accredited.[29]

Knowledgeable, articulate, and quick on the uptake, Mary Munford was her own best argument for taking female intellect seriously. During one legislative hearing, a delegate from Rockbridge County accused her of trying to drain money from the education of illiterate white children. Then Munford inquired of him,

> How many illiterate children there were in his own county of Rockbridge. He did not know. She told him: there were 234. She

asked him how many vacant seats there were in his county's schools. He did not know that either. She told him again: there were 1355. She then suggested that some of his professed enthusiasm for the education of children might be used in persuading his constituents to send their children to the schools which were already there.[30]

The Coordinate College League brought its proposal to the General Assembly in 1912, 1914, and again in 1916, and the sides became clear. Women were uniformly for it. As they could not vote, however, the question was how the men divided. The coordinate college drew support from a majority of the university's faculty and from a number of legislators. "Gentlemen," one of them explained as he opened a hearing, "as it happens, all of my boys are girls." The alumni, however, were generally opposed, and they conducted a hotly emotional campaign of their own.[31] All of their arguments were easily (and repeatedly) refuted by Mary Munford and her supporters, but this did not seem to matter. The alumni were sentimentally attached to the university as they had known it, and they resented any potential invasion of their ground. Ultimately, they spoke for maintaining one of Virginia's greatest symbols of male privilege.

In the 1916 session of the legislature, the coordinate college bill lost by a vote of forty-six to forty-eight. Although the league vowed to keep trying, it never again came so close to victory. The legislature, meanwhile, cleansed its conscience by enacting two bills of major importance. Women were admitted to the College of William and Mary in 1918, and women were admitted to the University of Virginia's graduate and professional programs in 1920.

For those who had ears to hear, the coordinate college fight was proof that women needed the vote. The exclusion of women from formal politics had been justified in the past by the code of chivalry: While women stayed above the sordid world of politics, men promised to protect women's interests. The coordinate college episode, however, showed that chivalry—in the world of politics, at least—was a sham. For the first time in history, Virginia women had defined their own interests and spoken with one voice. And the majority of men had refused to listen.

The idea that women should participate more fully in politics also gained plausibility from women's highly visible successes in business and in literature. Maggie Lena Walker was Virginia's outstanding businesswoman and a pivotal leader in Richmond's black community. Walker worked her way up; her mother had supported her family by taking in washing, and Maggie herself was pressed into service early—delivering clothes, marketing, and watching her younger brother. She was still able to attend school, though, and after graduating from normal school in 1883 she became a teacher. Not long after, she married and started a family of her own.

Maggie Walker meanwhile discovered a knack for business. At seventeen she was elected to office in the Independent Order of Saint Luke, a black fraternal society and insurance organization. At thirty-two Walker became head of the order ("Right Worthy Grand Secretary-Treasurer"), and from that day in 1899 the organization experienced spectacular growth. In twenty-five years the order grew from fifty-seven local chapters to fifteen hundred, acquired an office building and assets of almost four hundred thousand dollars, and increased its labor force from one lone clerk to a staff of fifty. Along the way, Walker also started a newspaper, the *Saint Luke Herald,* and in 1903 she founded the Saint Luke Penny Savings Bank. Serving as the bank's president until 1929, she is believed to have been the first woman bank president in the United States.[32]

Not far from the Saint Luke Bank, the Pin Money Pickle factory operated at full steam. The Pin Money Pickle company was the creation of Ellen Tompkins Kidd, who, like almost everyone else in the lean years after the Civil War, had cast about for some way to make ends meet. She began in her own kitchen with an old family recipe for sweet pickles. What set her apart from the scores of other small-time picklers and bakers and confectioners was her never-say-die marketing strategy. One of her techniques was to board a train and peddle her pickles among the passengers in the dining car; she returned from one such trip with several hundred dollars in orders. When Ellen Kidd retired in 1927, her company was doing an annual business of half a million dollars.[33]

There were still other success stories in turn-of-the-century Virginia; Amanda Ellen Thorp, for example, teamed up with partners in Richmond and opened Richmond's first movie theater, the Dixie, in 1907.[34] Like their predecessors in the eighteenth and nineteenth centuries, these women stood out as female achievers in a male world of business. Unlike their predecessors, they made it on their own. Maggie Walker, Ellen Kidd, and Amanda Thorp all had married, but not one of them relied on her husband for her start—or her advance—in business.

Finding one's own path was a requirement for women who pursued the solitary craft of writing. Mary Johnston's name became a household word in 1900 when she published *To Have and To Hold*, a romance set in seventeenth-century Jamestown. The book topped the best-seller list, and over the next ten years Johnston, who lived both in Richmond and in Bath County, brought out four more best-selling novels. In 1913, with *Hagar*, she turned to feminist fiction and so, in a subtler way, did her friend Ellen Glasgow. With the appearance of *Virginia*, also in 1913, Glasgow emerged as an American novelist of the first rank.

In their novels Mary Johnston and Ellen Glasgow explored both the weight of tradition and what Glasgow called the "struggle for the liberation of personality." *Hagar* was an attempt to imagine what liberation might look like. Hagar Ashendyne was a Virginia girl who refused to marry a man she did not love, who was thrown out of school for becoming secretly engaged to one of her professors (she didn't marry him, either), who became a writer, and who eventually escaped to New York City, where she flourished as a worker for women's rights and social justice. Having firmly established her own identity, Hagar was ready to find her man and was rewarded by the prompt appearance of a bridge builder who was also a feminist's dream. The novel ends happily with their engagement.[35]

Virginia was a study of tradition, a story of a woman who did exactly what her society expected of her. Virginia Pendleton Treadwell staked everything on love, giving herself up to exhausting sacrifice for her husband and children. In the end she emerged with nothing. Her husband became bored and deserted her; her grown children did not need her. "Speechless, inert, unseeing," she never came to terms with having "outlived her usefulness."[36]

In her later novels—most notably *Barren Ground* (1925), *The Sheltered Life* (1932), and *Vein of Iron* (1935)—Ellen Glasgow continued to probe the dilemmas of women victimized by a culture that demanded they be passive, dependent, and superficial. Glasgow's fascination with this theme did not find universal approval; her friend and rival James Branch Cabell in 1947 satirized it as "The Tragedy of Everywoman As It Was Lately Enacted in the Commonwealth of Virginia."[37] But Cabell did not appreciate how heavily the force of tradition weighed on Virginia's first feminists. His attitude might have been different had he recalled the fate of woman suffrage.

The Virginia woman suffrage movement was born in 1909 when a small group met to form the Equal Suffrage League. They elected Lila Meade Valentine their president, and although they expected a long siege, they went to work with high enthusiasm. Hoping to arouse the public and to win over the General Assembly, the suffragists developed a variety of campaign techniques. Some of them conquered their stage fright and learned to make speeches—from brightly decorated automobiles, from courthouse steps, on soapboxes if necessary. They canvassed house to house. They rented booths at county fairs. They held bake sales, both to raise money and to demonstrate their skill at housewifery. They distributed countless leaflets, supplied suffrage news to the press, and put out a newspaper of their own. They learned the political ropes, too. They did their homework, buttonholed legislators, and counted heads on crucial votes.

Like suffragists in other parts of the country, Virginia's suffragists advanced three main arguments. One was a matter of simple justice: Women were citizens, taxpayers, and rational human beings, just as men were, and therefore they deserved to vote, just as men did. Second, for all that women and men had in common, women still had special interests as women. Women needed the vote to protect their interests, especially since men were doing such a poor job of it.[38] Third, the world and the home were no longer separate places. In modern times, the government on every level had a direct impact on the home and the child; if the city allowed its water supply to become polluted, for example, there was nothing a mother could do to protect her children—unless she could vote. In order to be a good mother, then, the woman also had to be an active citizen. Moreover, the country needed the mother's touch. As novelist Mary Johnston put it, "I think when we have the mother sentiment in politics, the mother heart in business, the mother arm around the weak and helpless, . . . we will have better business, better politics, happier, healthier people and a bigger nobler world."[39]

When the United States entered World War I in 1917, the Equal Suffrage League temporarily suspended agitation for the vote and joined with dozens of other organizations, including the Virginia Association Opposed to Woman Suffrage, to support the war effort. As head of the Woman's Committee of the Council of National Defense, Mary Munford oversaw the labors of the state's white women. Margaret R. Johnson, of Richmond, chaired the parallel black organization, the Working Force of Negro Women.[40] Altogether, they performed miracles of mobilization.

Almost every homemaker in the state signed up to do her part for food production. There were meatless days and wheatless days. Planting a garden became a patriotic act. ("We do not say 'war gardens,' " Janie Porter Barrett commented, "and we are not quite sure about calling them 'peace gardens,' so we just say 'gardens.' ")[41] Canning classes were held everywhere. For fear that the absence of nurses and doctors might result in medical disaster among the civilian population, a massive public health drive was launched to teach the principles of preventive medicine. Women sold savings stamps and lined up thousands of subscribers for the Liberty Loans that financed the war. They collected tons of food and clothing for the relief of the war's victims in Europe. Last but not least, Virginia was a major staging area for the soldiers and sailors headed overseas. Virginia women therefore did extra duty in providing social services for "the boys" and family and friends who visited them in camp.[42]

All these contributions were grist for the suffrage mill; suffragists argued that the vote would be a just reward for women's wartime sacrifices. When Great Britain enfranchised women early in 1918, Virginia suffragists were delighted, and they were very proud in 1919 when Virginia-born Nancy Astor was elected Britain's first woman member of Parliament. In the United States, too, the movement was gathering momentum. In June 1919 Congress at last passed the Nineteenth Amendment to the Constitution and sent it on to the states for ratification.[43]

The Virginia Equal Suffrage League, by this time nearly twenty thousand strong, took up the ratification campaign with a will. But no amount of will or work could move the General Assembly. While a few of the legislators were warm supporters of the suffrage cause, the majority remained firmly opposed.

The stated issue was the "race question." Opponents of woman suffrage argued that the Nineteenth Amendment would enfranchise black women and thus pave the way for "Negro domination." At best, this was a false issue; suffragists found themselves responding (accurately, as it turned out) that with the poll tax and other restrictions in the 1902 state constitution, black women would register in no greater numbers than black men had. At their worst, opponents of woman suffrage resorted to some very low forms of racist demagoguery. When Carrie Chapman Catt, the distinguished president of the National American Woman Suffrage Association, appeared before the

General Assembly in 1920, an anonymous legislator blanketed the chamber with posters portraying Catt as a communist and an advocate of "social equality" between the races.[44] In the context of the times there was no deadlier slur. To the suffragists' credit they refused to get into the gutter with their opponents. It is not to their credit that they failed to take a more egalitarian stance.

In spite of the legislature's opposition, women in Virginia got the vote in 1920 when Tennessee became the thirty-sixth state to ratify the Nineteenth Amendment. (Virginia did not ratify until 1952.) Almost immediately some women entered mainstream politics. Mary Munford was appointed to the Democratic National Committee in 1920. In 1924 Kate Waller Barrett was a delegate to the Democratic National Convention, where she took the podium to nominate Carter Glass for president. (A New Jersey delegate liked her speech so much that he jumped up to nominate Barrett for vice-president.) Meanwhile, Sarah Lee Fain, of Norfolk, and Helen T. Henderson, representing Russell and Buchanan counties, took their seats as the first women ever elected to the General Assembly.[45]

It looked like a new era in politics, and women's organizations responded accordingly. The first task was to encourage women to register to vote. In Richmond this effort was headed among black women by Maggie Walker and community leader Ora Stokes. Among white women the registration drive was led by the League of Women Voters. When the Equal Suffrage League cheerfully went out of business in 1920, the League of Women Voters rose in its place to try to see to it that the new vote was an informed vote.[46]

While the league was nonpartisan, its members had some definite ideas about policy issues. The Virginia League of Women Voters collected thousands of signatures in support of international disarmament. Standing for streamlined government, the organization in 1921 inspired the governor to call the historic Conference on Governmental Efficiency. At the league's behest, the governor in 1921 appointed the Children's Code Commission, which in turn recommended the passage of twenty-four new laws. The legislative session of 1922 passed eighteen of the recommended bills, including a strong statute on child labor and a weaker one on compulsory education; "at least," league president Adèle Clark recalled, "it was a camel's foot in the tent."[47]

The League of Women Voters was only one of more than twenty women's organizations that had legislative concerns. In 1924 they teamed up to form an umbrella organization with the ungainly but accurate title of the Virginia Women's Council of Legislative Chairmen of State Organizations. The idea was to coordinate lobbying on any bill endorsed by three or more member organizations. In the 1926 session, for example, a bill to compel fathers to help support children born out of wedlock was endorsed by the Business and Professional Women's Clubs, the Council of Jewish Women, the Florence Crittenton Mission, the Home Economics Association, and the League of Women Voters, among others. The council monitored this and almost thirty other measures, and kept steady pressure on the legislature throughout the remainder of the 1920s.[48]

When the whole history of Virginia is one day written, Virginia women may well turn out to have constituted the single most progressive force during the period historians call the Progressive Era. But even at our present early stage of research, some important conclusions can be drawn. One is that Virginia women in the early twentieth century compiled a stunning record of public service. With supreme consistency, women who succeeded in business, the arts, or the professions devoted themselves in a significant way to reform or to community service. Maggie Walker, for example, organized the Council of Colored Women, and they in turn raised thousands of dollars for the Janie Porter Barrett School, for Richmond's first black visiting nurse, for a settlement house in Richmond, and for a tuberculosis sanitarium in Burkeville.[49]

Almost every other prominent woman of that day provided an additional example. Emily Chenault Runyon left her medical practice to serve as a medical missionary in China; after ill health dictated her return to the United States, she became involved in the public health movement. Orie Latham Hatcher resigned a professorship in the nation's most rigorous women's college (Bryn Mawr) to return to her home state and head the movement for greater educational opportunities for southern women. Anne Spencer, a poet whose work was published in the flowering of black culture known as the Harlem Renaissance, established Lynchburg's first lending library for blacks and helped found the local chapter of the National Association for the Advancement of Colored People. Ellen Kidd, of pickle-manufacturing fame, was an officer in the Equal Suffrage League, as were novelists Ellen Glasgow, Mary Johnston, and Kate Langley Bosher. And much of the work of the League of Women Voters was accomplished through the efforts of artists Adèle Clark and Nora Houston.[50]

Moreover, these women clearly had their own ideas about what was important. To a remarkable degree, women activists in the 1920s followed through on the promises the suffragists had made—promises to expand the electorate, to work for peace, to clean up government, and to protect the vulnerable. This was, as Mary Johnston had said, "the mother sentiment in politics." In part, this explains why Virginia politicians had refused to give women the vote in the first place: The men who ran "the Organization"—the dominant power in Virginia politics until the 1960s—were committed to a small electorate, to maintaining themselves in office, to promoting business, and to spending as little as possible on social programs.

Women activists, then, went against the grain; they refused to accept all the values of the powerful; they persisted in asking government to value children, motherhood, health, and education. This was doubly true of black women, who took up the added and more dangerous challenge of resisting white supremacy in an age of virulent racism and increasing segregation. They were altogether a remarkable generation. Their like would not be seen again until the 1970s.

•

For women in Virginia, as in the rest of the country, the late 1920s and 1930s were times of decelerating participation in public life. Nevertheless, Virginia could still boast some pathbreakers, and two of them led in the movement to preserve the traditions of Appalachian people. After more than a century of isolation, Virginians who lived in the mountains were finding their lives disrupted and transformed by large-scale lumbering and coal mining, by the building of roads, and by the stringing of electrical lines. Many mountaineers moved on—some to the mill towns of the piedmont, others to northern industrial cities, like generations of Virginians before them, looking for a better livelihood.

Laura Scherer Copenhaver and Annabel Morris Buchanan both lived in Marion, in southwest Virginia, and each in her own way moved to preserve folk traditions before it was too late. Copenhaver looked around her, saw a shortage of jobs and a surplus of wool, and launched Rosemont Craft industries. Having located older people who remembered the old hand-weaving techniques, she got them working together while she found buyers beyond Virginia's borders. Before long the coverlets, rugs, canopy covers, and tablecloths made by the Rosemont workers were world famous.[51]

For composer Annabel Morris Buchanan the incentive to action was the fear that old-time music was doomed to extinction. In the 1920s music was changing along with everything else in the mountains; recording company scouts discovered scores of performers who readily adapted their styles to reach a new mass market through records and radio. A few of them, like Texas Gladden and like Sara and Maybelle Carter of the famed Carter Family, achieved stardom. To Annabel Buchanan, however, the new country music (she called it "hillbilly whining") was a corruption of the authentic folk tradition. "I have become so suddenly and violently jealous of our southwest Virginia ballads and folk tunes," she wrote in 1931, "I can hardly think of anything now but getting them collected before they are all gone. . . . It makes me ill to think of the Romish Lady being lost."[52]

"The Romish Lady" and countless other songs were not only saved but made famous by the White Top Folk Festival. Organized chiefly by Buchanan in 1931, the first festival drew more than three thousand listeners, and when Eleanor Roosevelt attended in 1933 White Top became a household word. Throughout the depression decade, White Top was a focal point for musicians, collectors, and folklorists, and thanks largely to Annabel Morris Buchanan much of the rich folk heritage of the Virginia mountains was preserved.

Although activism became more difficult as the years passed, a number of other Virginia women carried the torch of progressivism into the late 1920s and 1930s. Naomi S. Cohn led a successful campaign in 1938 for a new law that shortened the employed woman's working day. In 1932 Lucy Randolph Mason became head of the National Consumers League, one of the country's most important advocacy groups for working women. Mason, who liked to let it be known that she was descended from *the* Randolphs and *the* Masons, later became a troubleshooter for the Congress of Industrial Organizations, helping to form labor unions in the South, "wherever or whenever and in whatever way."[53]

The major advocate of women employed in business, government, and the professions was the Federation of Business and Professional Women's Clubs; the federation was one of the first groups to endorse the Equal Rights Amendment after its initial introduction in 1923. The battle of the white-collar women, however, soon became a defensive battle. After the stock market crash of 1929, businesses retrenched and governments at all levels introduced measures that deliberately discouraged the employment of women. Elected president of the National Federation of Business and Professional Women in 1931, Geline MacDonald Bowman, of Richmond, led the fight against the new discrimination.[54]

The results were mixed. In the course of the New Deal, women headed a small fraction of the numerous new agencies designed to cope with the depression. Former suffrage organizer Eudora Ramsay Richardson was appointed supervisor of the Virginia Writers' Project, one of fourteen women to hold such positions nationwide. Ella Agnew, who had arrived in Blacksburg in 1914 as the nation's first home demonstration agent, organized the Women's Work Division to provide work relief for needy women.[55] At the same time, women were under great pressure to submerge their careers for the sake of those who allegedly needed the jobs more. In Virginia in 1936 only one-fifth of school districts would even consider the application of a married woman for a teaching position. In half of Virginia's districts, a teacher who married after she was employed was automatically fired.[56]

Then there was Pearl Harbor, and suddenly going out to work became a patriotic duty. The United States entered World War II late in 1941. Men joined the armed forces by the thousands, leaving their jobs vacant at the very time that demand for production was reaching an all-time high. Into the breach stepped the women. For many black women, this was their first opportunity to leave domestic service and to take on better-paying and less-lonely factory work. For both black and white women, this was an opportunity to show they could handle jobs that had formerly been monopolized by men. They performed well, and they were congratulated on all sides. In Lynchburg and Radford, for example, women had taken over men's jobs in foundries. "Ladies take a bow," their industry's magazine told them. "You are doing an expert double-barreled job of helping whip the Axis. . . . Foundrywomen, foundrymen salute you!"[57]

That was in 1943. A more pensive column in the same magazine dared to raise the question: Was this the beginning of a new era? Or was it "only a temporary expedient?" When the war ended in 1945, the short-term answer became clear. Women war workers were laid off in massive numbers, and after the plants retooled for peacetime production, the jobs went to returning GIs. As a well-orchestrated propaganda campaign made plain, women's new patriotic duty was to return home, cheerfully relinquishing jobs, skills, paychecks, and pride to the veterans.[58]

The back-to-the-home movement of the late 1940s and 1950s drew strength from anxieties similar to those that had helped produce the "true woman" ideal of the antebellum period. Having survived the disruptions of depression and war, learning to live with the tensions of the Cold War and the nuclear age, Virginians along with other Americans took comfort in an image of stable, happy families cared for by full-time wives and mothers. We do not yet know what parts women themselves played in the development of this image. We do know that the pressure to stay home was part of a long-term process by which women were discouraged from entering fully into public life.

The shift had begun in the 1920s, when the national political temper turned hostile to feminism and reform. The trend was furthered as many of Virginia's most prominent female public figures died or retired. During the depression and in the wake of World War II women were actively discouraged from following their career ambitions—and from having career ambitions. The finishing touch was what Betty Friedan called the "feminine mystique"—the idea that all women should find total fulfillment in marriage, motherhood, and homemaking.

To a considerable degree the pressure was effective. In the 1940s and 1950s, the legislative concerns of most Virginia women's organizations shrank. For several years the state League of Women Voters sank out of sight. From 1934 until 1953 not one woman was elected to the General Assembly. Women who embarked on professional careers faced a slippery slope. The proportion of Virginia college professors who were women declined steadily between 1930 and 1950. In none of the high-prestige professions did Virginia women advance steadily, decade by decade. During the 1950s the proportion of doctors who were women rose a little (from 5.3 percent to 5.8 percent), but the proportion of architects, clergy, and lawyers all declined.[59]

Whether they were in or out of the paid labor force, almost all Virginia women did housework. To the homemaker the twentieth century brought dazzling changes in household technology. Running water was a major advance. Electricity seemed like a miracle, although rural areas were slow to receive its benefits. In 1934 less than 8 percent of Virginia farms had electric power; by

1950 over 90 percent of Virginia's farms were electrified. Once the lines were in, the typical family would insist on lights first, a furnace second, and a cookstove next. In the towns, where the lines went up much earlier, women who could afford them bought the most popular appliances of the 1920s—the electric iron, the vacuum cleaner, and the electric washing machine. The freezer, the electric refrigerator, and the automatic washer followed in the 1950s, and the possibilities continued to multiply.[60]

The new inventions were called "laborsaving" devices, and they did indeed make housework less physically exhausting. Interestingly enough, they did not save time. Housewives in the 1960s spent as much time doing housework as their grandmothers had at the turn of the century, for with each new invention came a higher standard.[61] The real time-saver was birth control.

Relatively reliable and safe contraceptives (diaphragms and condoms) became available in the United States in the 1920s, and several groups of women set about making them more widely available in Virginia. The Virginia Federation of Women's Clubs supported two birth control clinics in the 1930s. The Richmond YWCA took action after one of its members nearly died from a mishandled abortion. As it happened, one of the board members was married to an employee of a rubber company. Blessed with a ready supplier, the YWCA quietly began distributing contraceptives to its members.[62]

While no device was problem free, the marketing of the IUD in the late 1950s and the birth control pill beginning in 1960 completed a contraceptive revolution. For the first time in history, women were able to decide whether and when they would bear children, and the consequences were momentous. The immediate impact was that the role of wife, mother, and homemaker became more appealing. While household appliances made housework less laborious, contraception saved women from the physical wear and tear of too many pregnancies, too close together; it allowed them to invest more time in each child; it offered the potential for greater satisfaction in sex. The back-to-the-home movement owed some of its persuasiveness to the fact that the home was a better place to be.

At the same time, contraception increased women's opportunities for activity outside the home, and so did the opening of thousands of new jobs. Once World War II was over, women were effectively barred from the "men's" jobs that so many of them had mastered during the war. But the postwar economy presented opportunities of its own, especially in clerical work, and Virginia women entered the paid labor force in a steadily widening stream. By 1970, 42 percent of Virginia women were employed outside the home. A large proportion of these women were married (42 percent), and over half of Virginia's gainfully employed women (58 percent) had children under the age of eighteen.[63]

And what of the feminine mystique? From the late 1940s through the 1960s, women were told time and again that they should be thoroughly fulfilled by marriage, motherhood, and homemaking. With each passing year, however, the feminine mystique was less applicable to the facts of women's daily lives. The mystique never settled many women's (not to mention men's) doubts about the real significance of unpaid labor in the home. Women in modern Virginia continued to do what they had done all along—to perform the essential life-supporting tasks of maintaining households and nurturing children and men. But in the twentieth century the true importance of these tasks became harder to appreciate, as the value of work was increasingly measured by the amount of money if brought in. Moreover, advertisements for new appliances devalued housework by making it look like push-button work that any fool could do. The phrase "just a housewife" became a common expression in the postwar era.

Nor could the feminine mystique speak to the fact that women were spending less of their lives mothering and more at work. Virginia women were living longer than ever before, while they were bearing an average of only two or three children. The typical woman completed her childbearing well before her thirtieth birthday, and she could look forward to twenty or thirty years of active life after her youngest child left home. What was she to do with that time? The idealization of the home supplied no answer. Perhaps most important, the emphasis on homemaking offered no support to the growing number of wives and mothers who held down paying jobs. For these women the feminine mystique functioned mainly as a source of guilt.

The times were contradictory; image and reality were increasingly out of phase with one another. By the late 1960s the need was acute for some new vision, a different way of understanding female experience, a new view of what women could do and be. The new image—or a set of new images—would soon be provided by the revival of feminism. But in order to launch a successful struggle for woman's rights, a climate conducive to the pursuit of human rights first had to exist.

The civil rights movement became front-page news in 1954 with the Brown decision, the United States Supreme Court's order to desegregate the public schools. Long before 1954, however, black Virginians had initiated numerous protests against racial discrimination, and they focused much of their attention on the educational system. In the 1920s black teachers in Richmond organized a public awareness campaign to draw attention to their paltry and clearly discriminatory salaries; despite their efforts and the best efforts of the Virginia Teachers Association, the salaries of black teachers at the end of the 1930s were still 30 percent less than those of white teachers. The teachers decided to sue. With the help of lawyers from the National Association for the Advancement of Colored People, Aline Black, a Norfolk high school teacher, sued her school board for a salary equal to that of similarly qualified whites.[64] Black lost the case and was fired from her job. Determination to challenge racism increased during World War II, however, as black Virginians took a full part in the fighting overseas and in the mobilization at home. As one woman recalled, "The unrest began during the war, and we sat in the front of the bus without the ability to express why we were doing it. The driver was very rude and said if we didn't move, the bus wouldn't. There was still so much fear in our hearts and we didn't want to be late for work, so we moved."[65]

The NAACP pursued a methodical assault on the legal foundations of segregation and in 1954 achieved a landmark victory with the Brown decision. In that decision the Supreme Court ruled that segregated facilities were inherently unequal and therefore unconstitutional. In Virginia, desegregation did go forward but not until 1959. Virginia's entire, rigidly segregated social structure was at stake, and while white Virginians held various opinions, the official policy was massive resistance. The General Assembly passed the key law in 1956: Any school under court order to integrate would automatically be closed by the governor. As it turned out, that was a price most parents were not willing to pay. After schools were actually closed in Front Royal, Charlottesville, Norfolk, and Prince Edward County, the massive resistance movement collapsed.[66]

No sooner was school desegregation begun than black activists launched a campaign to end segregation in every sort of public place. The technique used was the sit-in. Entering a segregated area, often a whites-only lunch counter, a group simply sat until they were either served or arrested, quietly braving whatever the consequences might be—heckling, jail sentences, beatings. The sit-ins were extremely effective. In March 1960 the nation was stunned by a *Life* magazine photograph of a fifty-eight-year-old grandmother being dragged away from a department store lunch counter by Richmond police. Downtown merchants were deeply embarrassed by the national exposure, and most retail stores desegregated shortly thereafter.[67]

The civil rights movement did not eliminate racism, but it did do away with some of the most visible and degrading forms of discrimination. Moreover, the movement brought about a renewed commitment to equality, an appreciation of the damage done by discrimination, and a new willingness to question old ideas about the worth of people who looked different. On every count, women as a group had a great deal to learn from this. In the middle 1960s they started to apply the lesson of the civil rights movement to themselves.[68]

The revival of feminism in Virginia probably dates from 1966, when the Commission on the Status of Women published its first report. Appointed at the behest of the federal government, commissions in every state uncovered evidence of persistent inequalities in almost every area of life. Virginia was no exception. In their report of 1966 and in reports issued periodically in the 1970s, the Virginia commissioners politely called attention to one problematic area after another. They discovered that Virginia was one of the few states with no law compelling fathers to help support children born out of wedlock. They discovered that for every preschooler enrolled in a day-care center, there were two others in need of day care but left out because the facilities simply were not there. The commissioners also discovered the full extent to which women were consigned to low-paying jobs. A study of state government employees, for example, showed that women held 62 percent of jobs paying less than $5,000 a year. But women held only 6 percent of jobs that paid $20,000 or more. For black women the statistics were more discouraging still. Black women held 23 percent of the jobs paying less than $5,000 and only 0.1 percent of the jobs paying $20,000 or more.[69]

The list went on and it expanded as more areas came under investigation. In 1977 more than thirteen hundred women from every part of the state came together for the Virginia Women's Meeting, a conference to discuss women's issues and to select delegates to the National Women's Conference to be held in Texas later that year. The range of topics was enormous. The Virginia Women's Meeting addressed the needs of homemakers, military wives, the poor (the majority of whom were women), and the elderly (the majority of whom were also women). The delegates discussed the particular problems and contributions of minority women. They discussed physical abuse and sexual assault. They talked about credit, housing, health care, social security, sexual preference, and sex-role stereotyping in the media. They dealt with women in education, athletics, the arts, and small business.[70]

The meeting was not without controversy, and heated debate erupted on two issues. One was abortion, a politically charged

topic since 1973, when the United States Supreme Court legalized abortion and made first-trimester abortions a matter of
individual conscience. The other was the Equal Rights Amendment. The amendment itself was brief and simple: "Equality of
rights under the law shall not be denied or abridged by the
United States or by any State on account of sex." (The remaining twenty-eight words of the amendment gave Congress the
power of enforcement and defined when the amendment would
take effect.)[71] Since the precise consequences could not be
predicted, the amendment proved a fertile field for argument.
Supporters of the ERA saw in it a chance to realize their best
hopes; opponents believed it would make a reality of their worst
fears.

On these two powerfully symbolic issues there was no consensus in sight as Virginia moved into the 1980s. Nevertheless,
increasing numbers of Virginians, both female and male, were
accepting the idea that women as a group had suffered from
unjust discrimination and that steps to remedy the situation
were in order. Increasing numbers of Virginians, in other
words, were becoming feminists.

From the vantage point of 1980, much had been begun, and
much remained to be done. Despite a good deal of noise about
affirmative action, 80 percent of gainfully employed women still
crowded the bottom of the occupational ladder, and the gap
between the average earnings of women and the earnings of men
actually grew worse in the two decades after 1960. Wives and
mothers in the labor force—and their numbers continued to
increase—faced the "double day"; after eight hours on the job,
most women still found themselves responsible for virtually all
the housework and child care. The fundamental character of
women's work proved highly resistant to change.

At the same time, Virginians by the early 1980s could point to
a number of important new developments. In 1970 in response
to a lawsuit, the University of Virginia opened its doors to
women undergraduates. In colleges and universities all over the
state, students and professors questioned the content of their
courses and books, and began to see that history, literature, and

a host of other studies looked different and richer once the female experience was taken into account. In the public schools athletic opportunities for girls increased dramatically. By 1983 more than forty programs for victims of domestic violence existed, and fourteen rape crisis centers assisted victims of sexual assault. After several years of lobbying on the part of women's groups and of study on the part of the State Crime Commission, the General Assembly in 1981 enacted a set of major reforms in the state's sexual assault laws.[72] The return of women to public life also showed in the composition of the legislature; more women served in the General Assembly in the four years from 1980 to 1983 (sixteen) than had served during the five decades between 1920 and 1970. In the 1980s, moreover, women won seats in the state Senate for the first time.[73]

How significant will all of this look one hundred years from now? Much depends on the answers to some basic questions. Will men be drawn into greater involvement in child care and housework? More than any other change, this one would seem to have the potential to bring about some long-overdue appreciation for the work that women have done all along. Will Virginia women continue to gain access to the world beyond their homes? The historical record suggests that caution is warranted; over the centuries women's access to the world beyond the home has advanced, then retreated. If women do continue their entry into public life, will they bring distinctive values with them? Will they be able to apply the "traditional" female values—compassion, cooperation, nurture, and service—to the public realm?

From the perspective of today, Virginia women appear to be in a strong position to influence the course of history, both in public policy and in day-to-day living in families and communities. What happens next, more than ever before, is up to them.

Short Titles and Symbols

CW	Colonial Williamsburg Foundation
Duke	Manuscript Department, William R. Perkins Library, Duke University, Durham, N.C.
Hampton	Hampton University Archives, Collis P. Huntington Memorial Library, Hampton University, Hampton, Va.
RTD	*Richmond Times-Dispatch*
UNC	Southern Historical Collection, Wilson Memorial Library, University of North Carolina, Chapel Hill
UVA	Manuscripts Department, University of Virginia Library, Charlottesville
VC	*Virginia Cavalcade,* published by the Virginia State Library since 1951
VCU	Special Collections and Archives, Tompkins-McCaw Library, Medical College of Virginia Campus of Virginia Commonwealth University, Richmond
VHS	Virginia Historical Society, Richmond
VMHB	*Virginia Magazine of History and Biography,* published by the Virginia Historical Society since 1893
VSL	Archives Branch, Virginia State Library, Richmond
VSU	Special Collections, Johnston Memorial Library, Virginia State University, Ettrick

W&M   Manuscripts Department, Earl Gregg Swem Library, College of William and Mary in Virginia, Williamsburg

WMQ   *William and Mary Quarterly,* published by the College of William and Mary in Virginia from 1892 to 1945, and by the Institute of Early American History and Culture since 1946

Notes

CHAPTER 1: "No Obey"

1. Gabriel Archer quoted in John R. Swanton, *The Indians of the Southeastern United States* (Washington, D.C., 1946), 643.

2. John Smith quoted in Warren M. Billings, ed., *The Old Dominion in the Seventeenth Century: A Documentary History of Virginia, 1606–1689* (Chapel Hill, 1975), 216. *See also* Christian F. Feest, "Virginia Algonquians," in Bruce G. Trigger, ed., *Handbook of North American Indians*, 15, *Northeast* (Washington, D.C., 1978), 253–270.

3. John Smith quoted in Billings, *Old Dominion*, 215. *See also* Swanton, *Indians of the Southeastern United States*, 273–277, 293–294, 306–307.

4. John Smith (first quotation) and William Strachey (second quotation) in Swanton, *Indians of the Southeastern United States*, 448, 710.

5. Henry Spelman quoted in ibid., 414.

6. William Strachey quoted in ibid., 710.

7. Edmund S. Morgan, *American Slavery, American Freedom: The Ordeal of Colonial Virginia* (New York, 1975), 51–56; John Smith quoted in Billings, *Old Dominion*, 215.

8. John Smith quoted in Billings, *Old Dominion*, 216.

9. Ibid., 215; James Axtell, ed., *The Indian Peoples of Eastern America: A Documentary History of the Sexes* (New York, 1981).

10. John Smith quoted in Frances Mossiker, *Pocahontas: The Life and the Legend* (New York, 1976), 80; Philip L. Barbour, "Pocahontas," in Edward T. James, Janet Wilson James, amd Paul S. Boyer, eds., *Notable American Women, 1607–1950: A Biographical Dictionary*, 3 vols. (Cambridge, Mass., 1971), 3:78–81; Barbour, *Pocahontas and Her World* (Boston, 1970).

11. Rayna Green, "The Pocahontas Perplex: The Image of Indian Women in American Culture," *Massachusetts Review* 16 (Autumn 1975): 698–714; Philip Young, "The Mother of Us All: Pocahontas Reconsidered," *Kenyon Review* 24 (Summer 1962): 391–415.

12. Gabriel Archer quoted in Charles Edgar Gilliam, "Queen Oppussoquionuske," *Tyler's Quarterly Historical and Genealogical Magazine* 23 (Jan. 1942): 150.

13. George Percy quoted in Morgan, *American Slavery, American Freedom,* 74.

14. Nancy Oestreich Lurie, "Indian Cultural Adjustment to European Civilization," in James Morton Smith, ed., *Seventeenth-Century America: Essays in Colonial History* (New York, 1959), 49–55.

15. Carolyn Thomas Foreman, *Indian Women Chiefs* (Muskogee, Okla., 1954), 31–32. Most historians have identified the recipient of the silver badge as "Queen Anne." Martha W. McCartney identifies Cockacoeske as its recipient and identifies Anne as Cockacoeske's niece and successor ("Cockacoeske," [unpublished paper, 1984]).

16. Virginia Ferrar to [Lady Berkeley], 10 Aug. 1650, Ferrar Papers, Box 7, no. 692 (vi), Magdalene College, Cambridge, Virginia Colonial Records Project microfilm, reel 573 (transcription by Jon Kukla), VSL.

17. Quoted in Julia Cherry Spruill, *Women's Life and Work in the Southern Colonies* (1938; reprint, New York, 1972), 9.

18. Mary Johnston, *To Have and To Hold* (Boston, 1900), 13–14, 20. *See also* Mrs. Henry Lowell [Minnie Gathright] Cook, "Maids for Wives," *VMHB* 50 (Oct. 1942): 300–320; *VMHB* 51 (Jan. 1943): 71–86.

19. Cary Carson and Lorena S. Walsh, "The Material Life of the Early American Housewife" *Winterthur Portfolio,* forthcoming.

20. James Horn, "Servant Emigration to the Chesapeake in the Seventeenth Century," in Thad W. Tate and David L. Ammerman, eds., *The Chesapeake in the Seventeenth Century: Essays on Anglo-American Society* (New York, 1979), 51–95.

21. Morgan, *American Slavery, American Freedom,* 127 (first quotation); Billings, *Old Dominion,* 136 (second quotation).

22. Spruill, *Women's Life and Work,* 321–323; Darrett B. and Anita H. Rutman, *A Place in Time: Middlesex County, Virginia, 1650–1750* (New York, 1984).

23. Nancy F. Cott, ed., *Root of Bitterness: Documents of the Social History of American Women* (New York, 1972), 32.

24. John Hammond, *Leah and Rachel, or, the Two Fruitfull Sisters Virginia and Mary-land: Their Present Condition, Impartially Stated and Related,* in Peter Force, comp., *Tracts and Other Papers, Relating Principally to the Origin, Settlement, and Progress of the Colonies in*

North America, from the Discovery of the Country to the Year 1776, 4 vols. (Washington, D.C., 1836–1846), vol. 3, no. 14, p. 12.

25. Carson and Walsh, "Material Life of the Early American Housewife."

26. Information on parental loss comes from Rutman and Rutman, *A Place in Time.* The other figures are borrowed from Maryland, but probably describe the Virginia situation with reasonable accuracy, as the colonies formed a single region. *See* Lois Green Carr and Lorena S. Walsh, "The Planter's Wife: The Experience of White Women in Seventeenth-Century Maryland," *WMQ*, 3d ser., 34 (Oct. 1977): 542–571.

27. Lois Green Carr, "Inheritance in the Colonial Chesapeake" (unpublished paper); Lorena S. Walsh, " 'Till Death Us Do Part': "Marriage and Family in Seventeenth-Century Maryland," in Tate and Ammerman, *The Chesapeake in the Seventeenth Century,* 126–152.

28. "Papers Relating to the Administration of Governor Nicholson and to the Founding of William and Mary College," *VMHB* 7 (Jan. 1900): 278.

29. Again, the estimate is for Maryland, as explained in note 26 above. *See* Lois Green Carr, cited by Walsh, " 'Till Death Us Do Part,' " 132.

30. Quoted in Billings, *Old Dominion,* 102.

31. Ibid., 95, 96 (second and third quotations); Morgan, *American Slavery, American Freedom,* 152 (first quotation).

32. Spruill, *Women's Life and Work,* 330–331.

33. Quoted in Lawrence John Spagnola, "The Witchcraft Cases of Maryland and Virginia, 1626–1712: A Study of Social Friction in the Chesapeake Colonies During the Seventeenth Century" (Honors thesis, Harvard College, 1977), 31.

34. Richard Beale Davis, "The Devil in Virginia in the Seventeenth Century," *VMHB* 65 (Apr. 1957): 147; Elizabeth Dabney Coleman, "The Witchcraft Delusion Rejected," *VC* 6 (Summer 1956): 28–34.

35. Spruill, *Women's Life and Work,* 236–241; Lois Green Carr, "Margaret Brent," in James et al., *Notable American Women,* 1:236–237.

36. Anne Cotton, *An Account of Our Late Troubles in Virginia,* in Force, *Tracts,* vol. 1, no. 9, p. 10.

37. Herbert R. Paschal, ed., "George Bancroft's 'Lost Notes' on the General Court Records of Seventeenth-Century Virginia," *VMHB* 91 (July 1983): 356 (quotation); Wilcomb E. Washburn, "The Humble

Petition of Sarah Drummond," *WMQ*, 3d ser., 13 (July 1956): 354–375.

38. Jane D. Carson, "Lady Frances Berkeley," in James et al., *Notable American Women*, 1:135–136.

39. Albert Edward McKinley, *The Suffrage Franchise in the Thirteenth English Colonies in America* (1905; reprint, New York, 1969), 35, 473–474.

40. T. H. Breen and Stephen Innes, *"Myne Owne Ground": Race and Freedom on Virginia's Eastern Shore, 1640–1676* (New York, 1980), 8–17.

41. Winthrop D. Jordan, *White Over Black: American Attitudes Toward the Negro, 1550–1812* (Baltimore, 1969).

42. Billings, *Old Dominion*, 161 (quotation); Morgan, *American Slavery, American Freedom*, 334–335.

43. Billings, *Old Dominion*, 172–174; Morgan, *American Slavery, American Freedom*, 312–313, 329–337.

CHAPTER 2: "Prepar'd for Compliance"

1. Klaus Wust, *The Virginia Germans* (Charlottesville, 1969).

2. "Boundary Line Proceedings, 1710," *VMHB* 5 (July 1897): 10.

3. Roberta Ingles Steele and Andrew Lewis Ingles, eds., *Escape from Indian Captivity: The Story of Mary Draper Ingles and Son Thomas Ingles As Told by John Ingles, Sr.*, 2d ed. (Radford, Va., 1982).

4. The story of Mad Anne Bailey is omitted here because of doubts as to its authenticity. *See* Grace McCartney Hall, "Anne Bailey in West Virginia Tradition," *West Virginia History* 17 (Oct. 1955): 22–79.

5. William K. Boyd, ed., *William Byrd's Histories of the Dividing Line Betwixt Virginia and North Carolina* (Raleigh, 1929), 314; Washington quoted in Julia Cherry Spruill, *Women's Life and Work in the Southern Colonies* (1938; reprint, New York, 1972), 41.

6. Edmund S. Morgan, *Virginians at Home: Family Life in the Eighteenth Century* (Williamsburg, 1952), 74–78.

7. Darrett B. and Anita H. Rutman, *A Place in Time: Middlesex County, Virginia, 1650–1750* (New York, 1984) (quotations); Cary Carson and Lorena S. Walsh, "The Material Life of the Early American Housewife" *Winterthur Portfolio*, forthcoming.

8. Rutman and Rutman, *A Place in Time*.

9. Deborah G. White, *Arn'n't I a Woman? Female Slaves in the Plantation South* (New York, 1985). *See also* James A. Rawley, *The Transatlantic Slave Trade: A History* (New York, 1981), and Allan

Kulikoff, *Tobacco and Slaves: The Development of Southern Cultures in the Chesapeake, 1680–1800* (Chapel Hill, 1986), for summaries of recent scholarship.

10. Allan Kulikoff, "The Origins of Afro-American Society in Tidewater Maryland and Virginia, 1700–1790," *WMQ*, 3d ser., 35 (Apr. 1978): 230.

11. Marion Tinling, "Cawsons, Virginia, in 1795–1796," *WMQ*, 3d ser., 3 (Apr. 1946): 283 (first quotation); Gerald W. Mullin, *Flight and Rebellion: Slave Resistance in Eighteenth-Century Virginia* (New York, 1972), 64 (second quotation).

12. Quoted in Mary Beth Norton, *Liberty's Daughters: The Revolutionary Experience of American Women, 1750–1800* (Boston, 1980), 87.

13. Kulikoff, "Origins of Afro-American Society," 245, 249–250.

14. Mullin, *Flight and Rebellion*, 40, 113–114; White, *Arn'n't I a Woman?*

15. Norton, *Liberty's Daughters*, 164 (first quotation); Mullin, *Flight and Rebellion*, 73 (second quotation).

16. Susan Burrows Swan, *Plain and Fancy* (New York, 1977), 12; Accession files, no. 2847, Museum of Early Southern Decorative Arts, Winston-Salem, N.C.; *Virginia Gazette* (Purdie), 21 Mar. 1766; *Virginia Gazette* (Purdie & Dixon), 20 Feb. 1772.

17. Quoted in Norton, *Liberty's Daughters*, 4.

18. Tinling, "Cawsons," 283, 285.

19. Quoted in Mildred K. Abraham, "The Library of Lady Jean Skipwith: A Book Collection from the Age of Jefferson," *VMHB* 91 (July 1983): 319.

20. Quoted in Norton, *Liberty's Daughters*, 35.

21. Quoted in Daniel Blake Smith, *Inside the Great House: Planter Family Life in Eighteenth-Century Chesapeake Society* (Ithaca, N.Y., 1980), 67–68.

22. Mildred Smith to Betsy Ambler, 1782 (quotation); Betsy Ambler Brent to Mildred Smith, 10 Jan. 1786, Eliza Jaquelin Ambler Papers, CW.

23. Spruill, *Women's Life and Work*, 164, 216 (first and second quotations); Norton, *Liberty's Daughters*, 61 (third quotation).

24. Suzanne Lebsock, *The Free Women of Petersburg: Status and Culture in a Southern Town, 1784–1860* (New York, 1984), 23, 56–57.

25. Quoted in Morgan, *Virginians at Home*, 49.

26. Spruill, *Women's Life and Work*, 348–349.

27. Ibid., 113–122.

28. Morgan, *Virginians at Home,* 17 (first quotation); Smith, *Inside the Great House,* 63 (second quotation).

29. Mullin, *Flight and Rebellion,* 114; Kenneth A. Lockridge, *Literacy in Colonial New England: An Enquiry into the Social Context of Literacy in the Early Modern West* (New York, 1974), 97.

30. Norton, *Liberty's Daughters,* 257–263; Smith, *Inside the Great House,* 61–68; Spruill, *Women's Life and Work,* 185–207, 255–259.

31. Abraham, "The Library of Lady Jean Skipwith"; Spruill, *Women's Life and Work,* 220 (quotation).

32. Eliza J. A. B. Carrington to Ann Ambler Fisher, Nov. 1810, Eliza Jaquelin Ambler Papers, CW.

33. Martha Washington to Frances Bassett Washington, 15 Sept. 1794, Mount Vernon Ladies' Association transcript of original in Huntington Library, San Marino, Calif.

34. Smith, *Inside the Great House,* 238–239, 246; Lorena S. Walsh, "The Experiences and Status of Women in the Chesapeake, 1750–1775" (unpublished paper, May 1983), 21.

35. Rutman and Rutman, *A Place in Time.*

36. *Return of the Whole Number of Persons within the Several Districts of the United States . . .* (Philadelphia, 1791), 50. By contrast, New York's population in 1790 was 33,000; Philadelphia's was 28,500; Boston's was 18,000; and Baltimore's was 13,500.

37. Quoted in Spruill, *Women's Life and Work,* 273.

38. Quoted in ibid., 296.

39. Suzanne Lebsock, "Women and Economics in Virginia: Petersburg, 1784–1820" (Ph.D. diss., University of Virginia, 1977), 225.

40. Spruill, *Women's Life and Work,* 283–284.

41. Ibid., 269 (quotation); Linda E. Speth, "Woman's Sphere: Role and Status of White Women in 18th Century Virginia" (Master's thesis, Utah State University, 1980), 53–55.

42. Spruill, *Women's Life and Work,* 265–266; Jane D. Carson, "Clementina Rind," in Edward T. James, Janet Wilson James, and Paul S. Boyer, eds., *Notable American Women, 1607–1950: A Biographical Dictionary,* 3 vols. (Cambridge, Mass., 1971), 3:161 (quotation).

43. *Virginia Argus* (Richmond), 27 Dec. 1799.

44. Speth, "Woman's Sphere," 52.

45. Spruill, *Women's Life and Work,* 288–289.

46. *Virginia Gazette* (Dixon & Hunter), 1 July, 23 Sept. 1775.

47. Spruill, *Women's Life and Work*, 266.
48. Quoted in Norton, *Liberty's Daughters*, 123.
49. On political thinkers in the revolutionary era and their failure to take women into account, *see* Linda K. Kerber, *Women of the Republic: Intellect and Ideology in Revolutionary America* (Chapel Hill, 1980), 15–32.
50. *Virginia Gazette* (Purdie), 27 July 1769 (quotation); Norton, *Liberty's Daughters*, 184.
51. Mrs. Vivian Minor [Emily White] Fleming, *Historic Periods of Fredericksburg, 1608–1861* (Richmond, 1921), 19–20 (first quotation); Spruill, *Women's Life and Work*, 271 (second quotation).
52. Deposition of Sarah Benjamin, 1837, in John C. Dann, ed., *The Revolution Remembered: Eyewitness Accounts of the War for Independence* (Chicago, 1980), 244–245.
53. Charles Campbell, "Reminiscences of the British at Bollingbrook," *Southern Literary Messenger* 6 (Jan. 1840): 85–88.
54. Betsy Ambler to Mildred Smith, 1781, Eliza Jaquelin Ambler Papers, CW.
55. Norton, *Liberty's Daughters*, 209–212.
56. Louise Belote Dawe and Sandra Gioia Treadway, "Hannah Lee Corbin: The Forgotten Lee," *VC* 29 (Autumn 1979): 70–77.
57. Martha Washington to Fanny Bassett Washington, 25 Feb. 1788, Mount Vernon Ladies' Association, Mount Vernon, Va.; Martha Washington to Fanny Bassett Washington, 22 Oct. 1789, Mount Vernon Ladies' Association transcript of original in Etting Collection, Historical Society of Pennsylvania, Philadelphia.
58. Quoted in Norton, *Liberty's Daughters*, 190.

CHAPTER 3: "True Women"

1. Luther Porter Jackson, *Free Negro Labor and Property Holding in Virginia, 1830–1860* (New York, 1971), 172 (quotations); Tommy L. Bogger, "The Slave and Free Black Community in Norfolk, 1775–1865" (Ph.D. diss., University of Virginia, 1976), 49; Suzanne Lebsock, *The Free Women of Petersburg: Status and Culture in a Southern Town, 1784–1860* (New York, 1984), 95.
2. *Aggregate Amount of Persons within the United States in the Year 1810* (Washington, D.C., 1811).
3. Jackson, *Free Negro Labor*, 3–33.
4. Ruth Coder Fitzgerald, *A Different Story: A Black History of Fredericksburg, Stafford, and Spotsylvania, Virginia* (Greensboro,

N.C., 1979), 63; Lebsock, *Free Women of Petersburg*, 93–94 (quotation).

5. Fitzgerald, *A Different Story*, 73–74; Jackson, *Free Negro Labor*, 20.

6. Lebsock, *Free Women of Petersburg*, 87–111, 97 (quotation).

7. Ibid., 98–99 (first quotation); Jackson, *Free Negro Labor*, 132, 156; John H. Russell, *The Free Negro in Virginia, 1619–1865* (New York, 1969), 154 (second quotation).

8. Jackson, *Free Negro Labor*, 191 (quotation); Lebsock, *Free Women of Petersburg*, 96, 98.

9. Petition "of the Subscribers Female and male Inhabitants," 21 Dec. 1803, Legislative Petitions, Fredericksburg, 1800–1852, General Assembly, VSL. *See also* Linda K. Kerber, *Women of the Republic: Intellect and Ideology in Revolutionary America* (Chapel Hill, 1980), 269–288.

10. Female Orphan Society of Norfolk Minute Book, 1816–1853, UVA; *Constitution and By-Laws of the Female Humane Association of the City of Richmond, with Sketch of the Association* (Richmond, 1898); Lebsock, *Free Women of Petersburg*, 196–212; Mary G. Powell, *The History of Old Alexandria, Virginia: From July 13, 1749 to May 24, 1861* (Richmond, 1928), 156.

11. Herbert T. Ezekiel and Gaston Lichtenstein, *The History of the Jews of Richmond from 1769 to 1917* (Richmond, 1917), 231.

12. *Richmond Enquirer*, 18 Nov. 1808 (first quotation); *Petersburg Republican*, 31 Dec. 1816 (second quotation).

13. William M. E. Rachal, "Virginia's First College for Women: The Female Collegiate Institute in Buckingham County," *VC* 2 (Summer 1952): 44–47; broadside, 1854[?], Abner Johnson Leavenworth and Frederick P. Leavenworth Papers, Duke.

14. Mary Isabella Blackford to Mary B. Blackford, 19 Feb., 26 June 1858, Blackford Family Papers, UNC.

15. Catherine Clinton, *The Plantation Mistress: Woman's World in the Old South* (New York, 1982), 123 (first quotation); Petersburg Franklin Society Minutes, 22 Mar. 1822, Duke (second quotation).

16. Virginia Cary, *Letters on Female Character, Addressed to a Young Lady, on the Death of Her Mother* (Richmond, 1828), 149.

17. T. V. Moore, *Adaptation of Religion to Female Character: A Discourse to Young Ladies, Delivered in the First Presbyterian Church, Richmond, Virginia, February 29th, 1852* (Richmond, 1852), 4. *See*

also Barbara Welter, "The Cult of True Womanhood: 1820–1860," *American Quarterly* 18 (Summer 1966): 151–174.

18. Cary, *Letters on Female Character*, 22.

19. Quoted in Edmund S. Morgan, *Virginians at Home: Family Life in the Eighteenth Century* (Williamsburg, 1952), 31.

20. Jan Lewis, *The Pursuit of Happiness: Family and Values in Jefferson's Virginia* (Cambridge, Eng., 1983), 198 (first quotation); Fanny Bernard to George S. Bernard, 3 Mar. 1856, Bernard Family Papers, UVA.

21. Anna Campbell diary, 23 Apr. 1851, Charles Campbell Papers, W&M.

22. Andrew B. Davidson, *Religion, the Best Accomplishment: A Sermon Preached to the Young Ladies of Harrisonburg, January 24th, 1813* (Harrisonburg, Va., 1813), 32–33.

23. Ibid., 19; Cary, *Letters on Female Character*, 24; Moore, *Adaptation of Religion*, 9.

24. John Holt Rice, *A Sermon to Young Women* (Richmond, 1819), 6.

25. Emelia Hunter to Mrs. Sprigg, n.d., Mercer Family Papers, VHS.

26. Samuel K. Jennings, *The Married Lady's Companion, or, Poor Man's Friend; in Four Parts* (Richmond, n.d.). *See also* Janet Bogdan, "Care or Cure? Childbirth Practices in Nineteenth-Century America," *Feminist Studies* 4 (June 1978): 92–99.

27. Eliza Ruffin Cocke to Mary C. Ruffin, n.d., Harrison Henry Cocke Papers, UNC.

28. Mary B. Blackford to Charly Blackford, 21 Sept. 1841, Blackford Family Papers, UNC.

29. Mary B. Blackford to Launcelot Blackford, 31 July 1848, Blackford Family Papers.

30. Julia Cherry Spruill, *Women's Life and Work in the Southern Colonies* (1938; reprint, New York, 1972), 250; Society of Friends, Quaker Records, 2:16–17, Valentine Museum transcripts of originals in the possession of the Orthodox Friends, Baltimore, Md. For non-Quaker women, *see* Joan R. Gundersen, "The Non-Institutional Church: The Religious Role of Women in Eighteenth-Century Virginia," *Historical Magazine of the Protestant Episcopal Church* 51 (Dec. 1982): 347–357.

31. *Petersburg Republican*, 29 Mar. 1843.

32. Gillfield Baptist Church Record Book 3, 19 Dec. 1858, 16 Jan., 17 July 1859, UVA.

33. Quoted in Clinton, *The Plantation Mistress,* 181–182.

34. Irving Brant, "Dolley Payne Todd Madison," in Edward T. James, Janet Wilson James, and Paul S. Boyer, eds., *Notable American Women, 1607–1950: A Biographical Dictionary,* 3 vols. (Cambridge, Mass., 1971), 2:483–485; Conover Hunt-Jones, *Dolley and the Great Little Madison* (Washington, D.C., 1977).

35. Emelia Hunter letter, n.d., Mercer Family Papers, VHS.

36. Sarah Kemp to William Kemp, 8 Nov. 1814, William Kemp Papers, Duke.

37. Anna Maria Garretson to Isaac Garretson, 10 May 1817, 20 Apr. 1822, Anna Maria Garretson Papers, UNC.

38. Quoted in Lebsock, *Free Women of Petersburg,* 73.

39. Ibid., 125–135.

40. *Supplement to the Revised Code of the Laws of Virginia* (Richmond, 1833), 222–223.

41. Cary, *Letters on Female Character,* 117; Mildred Smith to Betsy Ambler, June[?] 1780, Eliza Jaquelin Ambler Papers, CW.

42. Eliza Ruffin diary, n.d.; Eliza Ruffin Cocke to Tarissa Cocke, 24 Jan. 1848[?], Harrison Henry Cocke Papers, UNC.

43. Charles L. Perdue, Jr., Thomas E. Barden, and Robert K. Phillips, eds., *Weevils in the Wheat: Interviews with Virginia Ex-Slaves* (Bloomington, Ind., 1980).

44. Ibid., 48–49.

45. Robert Seager II, "Julia Gardiner Tyler," in James et al., *Notable American Women,* 3:494–496.

46. Lebsock, *Free Women of Petersburg,* 137–138.

47. Perdue et al., *Weevils in the Wheat,* 190.

48. Ann T. Davis to Robert Davis, 5 Dec. 1859, Beale-Davis Papers, UNC; Anne Firor Scott, *The Southern Lady: From Pedestal to Politics, 1830–1930* (Chicago, 1970), 22–53; Scott, *Making the Invisible Woman Visible* (Urbana, Ill., 1984), 175–189.

49. C. W. Andrews, *Memoir of Mrs. Anne R. Page* (Philadelphia, 1844); Marie Tyler McGraw, "Northern Virginia Colonizationists," *Northern Virginia Heritage* 5 (Feb. 1983): 9–10, 16, 18.

50. R. R. Gurley to Mary B. Blackford, 21 Jan. 1837, Blackford Family Papers, UNC; Carl N. Degler, *The Other South: Southern Dissenters in the Nineteenth Century* (New York, 1974), 33–36; L.

Minor Blackford, *Mine Eyes Have Seen the Glory* (Cambridge, Mass., 1954).

51. Philip S. Foner and Josephine F. Pacheco, *Three Who Dared: Prudence Crandall, Margaret Douglass, Myrtilla Miner—Champions of Antebellum Black Education* (Westport, Conn., 1984).

52. "Memorial of the Subscribing females," 19 Jan. 1832, Legislative Petitions, Augusta County, 1825–1833, General Assembly, VSL.

53. Quoted in Fitzgerald, *A Different Story*, 85.

CHAPTER 4: "Never Was No Time . . ."

1. Jefferson Davis, *The Rise and Fall of the Confederate Government* (New York, 1881).

2. Margaret Stanly Beckwith, "Reminiscences, 1844–1865," 2:9, VHS; Mrs. Roger A. [Sarah Agnes Rice] Pryor, *Reminiscences of Peace and War* (New York, 1904), 131.

3. Leon F. Litwack, *Been in the Storm So Long: The Aftermath of Slavery* (New York, 1980), 108–109.

4. Mary Ann Whittle to Lewis Neale Whittle, 20 Sept. 1861, Lewis Neale Whittle Papers, UNC; Robert Francis Engs, *Freedom's First Generation: Black Hampton, Virginia, 1861–1890* (Philadelphia, 1979), 41.

5. Bessie Callender to John E. Meade, 21 May 1861, Ruffin-Meade Papers, UNC; Kate D. Spaulding quoted in Beckwith, "Reminiscences, 1844–1865," 1:44, 54, VHS; Mary D. Robertson, ed., *Lucy Breckinridge of Grove Hill: The Journal of a Virginia Girl, 1862–1864* (Kent, Ohio, 1979), 132–133.

6. Thomas Robson Hay, "Belle Boyd," in Edward T. James, Janet Wilson James, and Paul S. Boyer, eds., *Notable American Women, 1607–1950: A Biographical Dictionary*, 3 vols. (Cambridge, Mass., 1971), 1:215–217; Ruth Scarborough, *Belle Boyd: Siren of the South* (Macon, Ga., 1983); Lucy Gaylord Starnes, "Girl Spy of the Valley," *VC* 10 (Spring 1961): 35–40.

7. James H. Bailey, "Crazy Bet, Union Spy," *VC* 1 (Spring 1952): 14–17; H. L. Trefousse, "Elizabeth L. Van Lew," in James et al., *Notable American Women*, 3:508–510.

8. Pryor, *Reminiscences*, 161.

9. Mary Elizabeth Massey, *Bonnet Brigades* (New York, 1966), 84–85.

10. Minutes of the Ladies Club of Washington Street Church, Petersburg, for Soldiers Relief, Charles Campbell Papers, W&M; C. Vann Woodward, ed., *Mary Chesnut's Civil War* (New Haven, 1981), 167.

11. Massey, *Bonnet Brigades*, 147.

12. Phoebe Yates Pember, *A Southern Woman's Story: Life in Confederate Richmond* (Jackson, Tenn., 1959), 156.

13. Ibid., 153, 157, 158, 183.

14. Elizabeth Dabney Coleman, "The Captain Was a Lady," *VC* 6 (Summer 1956): 35–41.

15. Bessie Callender to John E. Meade, 17 Oct. 1861, Ruffin-Meade Papers, UNC.

16. Massey, *Bonnet Brigades*, 147–148.

17. Michael B. Chesson, "Harlots or Heroines? A New Look at the Richmond Bread Riot," *VMHB* 92 (Apr. 1984): 131–175; Sara M. Evans, "Women at War: The Richmond Bread Riot, April 2, 1863" (unpublished paper), 10, 20.

18. Mary Elizabeth Massey, *Ersatz in the Confederacy* (Columbia, S.C., 1952).

19. John W. Wayland, ed., *Men of Mark and Representative Citizens of Harrisonburg and Rockingham County, Virginia* (Staunton, Va., 1943), 225.

20. Engs, *Freedom's First Generation*, 13, 26, 38, 47, 49.

21. Quoted in Massey, *Bonnet Brigades*, 209.

22. Robertson, *Lucy Breckinridge*, 80; Woodward, *Mary Chesnut's Civil War*, 591.

23. Quoted in Myron Berman, *Richmond's Jewry, 1769–1976: Shabbat in Shockoe* (Charlottesville, 1979), 196–197.

24. Quoted in Litwack, *Been in the Storm So Long*, 171.

25. Lance G. E. Jones, *The Jeanes Teacher in the United States, 1908–1933: An Account of Twenty-five Years' Experience in the Supervision of Negro Rural Schools* (Chapel Hill, 1937), 22–38.

26. "Rosa D. Bowser: Talent to Spare, Talent to Share," *Richmond Literature and History Quarterly* 1 (Fall 1978): 45–46; Lucy F. Simms to Dr. Frissell, 4 Jan. 1904, Lucy F. Simms Papers, Hampton; " 'Miss Lucy' Remembered," *Harrisonburg Daily News-Record*, 2 July 1980.

27. Engs, *Freedom's First Generation*, 148–149; M. F. Armstrong and Helen W. Ludlow, *Hampton and Its Students* (New York, 1875), 127–158, 166.

28. Peabody clippings, no. 127, Hampton.

29. *Financial Report, Donors' List, and Statement of Current Needs* (n.p., 1910).

30. *Washington Star*, 5 Feb. 1907.

31. Edgar A. Toppin, "V.S.U. Centennial Chronology," in Bruce Twyman, ed., *Virginia State University Centennial Celebration and Annual Founder's Day Observance* (n.p., 1982).

32. Charles E. Wynes, *Race Relations in Virginia, 1870–1902* (Charlottesville, 1961); *The University of Virginia News Letter*, 1 Nov. 1926.

33. Bell Irvin Wiley, *The Plain People of the Confederacy* (Baton Rouge, 1943), 83. *See also* Eugene D. Genovese, *Roll, Jordan, Roll: The World the Slaves Made* (New York, 1974), 97–112; James L. Roark, *Masters Without Slaves: Southern Planters in the Civil War and Reconstruction* (New York, 1977).

34. Bureau of Refugees, Freedmen, and Abandoned Lands of Virginia, 3945—Proceedings (no. 147), 22 Dec. 1865, Record Group 105, National Archives, Washington, D.C.

35. Crandall A. Shifflett, *Patronage and Poverty in the Tobacco South: Louisa County, Virginia, 1860–1900* (Knoxville, Tenn., 1982), 18–19, 52–53.

36. "Tents Make a Big Increase," *Norfolk Journal and Guide*, 9 June 1917; Woman's Work Exchange of Norfolk, Virginia, *Constitution and By-laws* ([Norfolk], n.d.); "Woman's-Exchange," [Charlottesville], broadside, VHS; "The Woman's Exchange," [Richmond], VHS; Woman's Exchange of Lynchburg, Records, 1890-1894, Accession 21419, Organization Records, VSL. For information on the Knights of Labor, we are indebted to Sue Levine.

37. U.S. Bureau of the Census, *Special Reports: Occupations at the Twelfth Census* (Washington, D.C., 1904), 406.

38. William D. Henderson, " 'A Great Deal of Enterprise': The Petersburg Cotton Mills in the Nineteenth Century," *VC* 30 (Spring 1981): 176–185; Henderson, "The Evolution of Petersburg's Economy, 1860–1900" (unpublished paper, 1983).

39. Anthelia Holt to Lottie V. Clark, 21 Sept. 1889, Lottie V. Clark Papers, W&M.

40. Holt to Clark, 26 Apr. 1889, 14 and 25 Feb., 2 Mar. 1892, Clark Papers.

41. Holt to Clark, 26 Apr. 1889, Clark Papers.

42. Katharine Spicer Edmonds, "In the Realm of Hospitality: Cookbooks of the Eastern Shore," *VC* 23 (Spring 1974): 14; Samuel A. Mann diary, 2, 3, and 10 May 1878, Samuel A. Mann Papers, VSU.

43. Shifflett, *Patronage and Poverty,* 97.

44. Suzanne Lebsock, *The Free Women of Petersburg: Status and Culture in a Southern Town, 1784–1860* (New York, 1984), 191–194. *See also* Etta Rebecca Williams, "Fannie Criss: Turn of the Century Dressmaker," *Richmond Quarterly* 4 (Spring 1982): 46–48.

45. *Report on the Population of the United States at the Eleventh Census: 1890. Part 2* (Washington, D.C., 1897), 718.

46. Lebsock, *Free Women of Petersburg,* 176–177, 191.

47. Margaret Husted, "Mary Randolph's *The Virginia Housewife:* America's First Regional Cookbook," *VC* 30 (Autumn 1980): 76–87.

48. Merritt Cross, "Mary Virginia Hawes Terhune," in James et al., *Notable American Women,* 3:439–441; Dorothy McInnis Scura, "Constance Cary Harrison: A Spirited Lady of Letters," *Richmond Literature and History Quarterly* 1 (Winter 1978): 16–20; Welford Dunaway Taylor, *Amélie Rives (Princess Troubetzkoy)* (New York, 1973); Benjamin Quarles, "Elizabeth Keckley," in James et al., *Notable American Women,* 2:310–311.

· 49. Willia Estelle Daughtry, "Sissieretta Jones: A Study of the Negro's Contribution to Nineteenth Century American Concert and Theatrical Life" (Ph.D. diss., Syracuse University, 1967); Sarah S. Hughes, "Portsmouth Musicians," in Jane H. Kobelski, ed., *Readings in Black and White: Lower Tidewater Virginia* (Portsmouth, Va., 1982), 49–50; Jane Braddick Peticolas file, Valentine Museum, Richmond; William R. Sargent, "The Quarles Portraits: Susannah Nicholson, Painter (1804–1858)" (Master's thesis, Marshall University, 1978).

50. L. Rees Watkins, *They Made It Happen: A Memorial to Carrie McGeorge Burke, 1883–1971* (Richmond, n.d.), 17–26.

51. R. Pierce Beaver, "Lottie Digges Moon," in James et al., *Notable American Women,* 2:570–571.

52. Ibid., 570.

53. Undated clipping provided by Evelyn Edwards, Richmond Chapter of Epicureans, Inc., Folder 279, Box 22, Accession 32425, Virginia Women's Cultural History Project, Inc., Papers, Organization Records, VSL.

54. *RTD,* 9 June 1940; W. W. Parker, *The Woman's Place. Her*

Position in the Christian World. The Problem Considered Under Four Grand Heads—Woman Outstripped by Man, Even in Domestic Handiwork (Richmond, 1892), 9. On women physicians, *see also* Rosalie Slaughter Morton, *A Woman Surgeon: The Life and Work of Rosalie Slaughter Morton* (New York, 1937).

55. *RTD,* 22 Oct. 1950; *Acts and Joint Resolutions Passed by the General Assembly of the State of Virginia, During the Session of 1891–92* (Richmond, 1892), 209; *Acts and Joint Resolutions Passed by the General Assembly of the State of Virginia, During the Session of 1895–96* (Richmond, 1895), 49.

56. Edward C. Burks, *President's Address Delivered at the Third Annual Meeting . . . Virginia State Bar Association* (Richmond, 1891).

57. Eliza Ruffin diary, 10–12, 19, 20, 26–27, Harrison Henry Cocke Papers, UNC.

58. Mary B. Blackford to Lucy L. Minor, 18 Jan. 1854, Blackford Family Papers, UNC.

59. Eleanor Flexner, *Century of Struggle: The Woman's Rights Movement in the United States* (New York, 1971), 113–130, 176; Anne Firor Scott and Andrew MacKay Scott, *One Half the People: The Fight for Woman Suffrage* (Urbana, Ill., 1983), 166.

60. "Education in Virginia," Jan. 1905, Mary-Cooke Branch Munford Papers, 1905–1930, Accession 28142, Personal Papers Collection, VSL.

61. Bailey, "Crazy Bet, Union Spy," 17.

62. Orra Langhorne, *Southern Sketches from Virginia, 1881–1901,* ed., Charles E. Wynes (Charlottesville, 1964).

63. Edward D. Jervey, "Elmina Slenker: Freethinker and Sex Radical," *Virginia Social Science Journal* 16 (Apr. 1981): 1–12.

64. Memorial Society of the Ladies of the City of Petersburg, Records, 1866–1912, p. 1 (6 May 1866), Accession 24254, Organization Records, VSL. *See also* Ladies Memorial Association of Appomattox Minutes, VHS.

65. Memorial Society of the Ladies of the City of Petersburg, Records, p. 9 (12 July 1867), p. 38 (7 Mar. 1868).

CHAPTER 5: "Struggle for the Liberation of Personality"

1. Nancy Astor quoted in Christopher Sykes, *Nancy: The Life of Lady Astor* (London, 1972), 29; Mark Sullivan quoted in Lois W. Banner, *American Beauty* (New York, 1983), 154.

2. *Fourteenth Annual Catalogue of the Officers and Students of Hartshorn Memorial College, Richmond, Virginia* (Richmond, 1897), 32.

3. Rosalind Rosenberg, *Beyond Separate Spheres: Intellectual Roots of Modern Feminism* (New Haven, 1982), 5–12; Frances J. Niederer, *Hollins College: An Illustrated History* (Charlottesville, 1973), 50 (quotation).

4. *Richmond Times*, 16 Dec. 1894.

5. Mrs. White M. [Jessie D.] Ryburn, Ellen S. Bowen, and Mrs. J. W. Walker, *Women of Old Abingdon* (Pulaski, Va., 1937), 13, 16–17.

6. *Annual Report of the Woman's Christian Temperance Union of Virginia* (Winchester, Va., 1888), 11.

7. Ibid.

8. *Eighth Annual Report of the Woman's Christian Temperance Union of Virginia* (Harrisonburg, Va., 1890), 27; *Tenth Annual Report of the Woman's Christian Temperance Union of Virginia* (Leesburg, Va., 1892), 11.

9. *Tenth Annual Report of WCTU*, 10; Anne Firor Scott, *The Southern Lady: From Pedestal to Politics, 1830–1930* (Chicago, 1970), 145–150.

10. Wallace Evan Davies, "Ann Pamela Cunningham," in Edward T. James, Janet Wilson James, and Paul S. Boyer, eds., *Notable American Women, 1607–1950: A Biographical Dictionary*, 3 vols. (Cambridge, Mass., 1971), 1:416–417; Elswyth Thane, *Mount Vernon Is Ours: The Story of Its Preservation* (New York, 1966).

11. Janet C. Kimbrough, "The Early History of the Association for the Preservation of Virginia Antiquities: A Personal Account," *VC* 30 (Autumn 1980): 68–75; Pamela Sparrow Williamson, *Brief Summary of the History of the National Society of the Colonial Dames of America and in the Commonwealth of Virginia* (n.p., 1961).

12. Herbert T. Ezekiel and Gaston Lichtenstein, *The History of the Jews of Richmond from 1769 to 1917* (Richmond, 1917), 232–233.

13. Walter Russell Bowie, *Sunrise in the South: The Life of Mary-Cooke Branch Munford* (Richmond, 1942), 49; Etta Belle Walker Northington, *A History of the Virginia Federation of Women's Clubs, 1907–1957* (Richmond, 1958), 11.

14. Peabody clippings, Hampton. The clipping (undated) on the Lunenburg case gave no further details.

15. Sadie Daniel St. Clair, "Janie Porter Barrett," in James et al.,

Notable American Women, 1:96–97; Janie Porter Barrett, *Locust Street Social Settlement, Hampton, Virginia* (Hampton, Va., 1912).

16. *Fourth Annual Report of the Industrial Home School for Colored Girls* (n.p., 1919), 20; *Twenty-Third Annual Report of the Virginia Industrial School for Colored Girls* (n.p., 1938), 11.

17. Kate Waller Barrett, "Some Reminiscences," Kate Waller Barrett Papers, UVA; Carol L. Urness, "Kate Harwood Waller Barrett," in James et al., *Notable American Women*, 1:97–99.

18. Unidentified clipping, Kate Waller Barrett Papers, 1:62; Kate Waller Barrett, "The Unmarried Mother and Her Child," Kate Waller Barrett Papers, UVA.

19. June Peterson, "Dr. Kate Waller Barrett: A Friend of Girls" (Master's thesis, University of Seattle, 1969); Otto Wilson, *Life of Dr. Kate Waller Barrett* (New York, 1974).

20. Quoted in Betsy Brinson, " 'Helping Others to Help Themselves': The Early History of the Richmond YWCA," 4, Richmond Young Women's Christian Association Archives, Richmond, Va.

21. Mrs. Ralph R. [Naomi C.] Chappell and Mrs. J. W. S. [Ellen V.] Gilchrist, "A History of the Y.W.C.A. of Richmond, Virginia, 1887–1937," VHS; *Fiftieth Annual Meeting of the Young Women's Christian Association* (Richmond, 1938); Lucy R. Mason to Anne Pridmore, 26 Mar. 1940, Lucy Randolph Mason Papers, Duke.

22. *Woman's Times* (special ed., *Richmond Times*), 30 May 1895; Nita Ligon Morse and Eda Carter Williams, *The History of Sheltering Arms Hospital: The First 75 Years, 1889–1964* (n.p., n.d.).

23. *Norfolk Virginian-Pilot*, 75th Anniversary ed., 26 June 1940; "Public Health Nursing in Virginia" (typescript), Virginia Nurses' Association Papers, VCU.

24. Anne F. Parsons, "Sadie Heath Cabaniss, Virginia's Pioneer Nurse"; Rose Z. Van Vort, "Recollections of Miss Cabaniss"; Nannie J. Minor, "The Nurses Settlement of Richmond, Virginia"; all in Virginia Nurses' Association Papers.

25. Nannie J. Minor manuscript (quotation); Minor, "Nurses Settlement"; Juanita Woods, "History of I.V.N.A."; all in Virginia Nurses' Association Papers.

26. William Allen Link, "Public Schooling and Social Change in Rural Virginia, 1870–1920" (Ph.D. diss., University of Virginia, 1981), 103–113; Kate Coles to Margaret Minor Bryan, Fall 1914[?], Kate (Flanagan) Coles Papers, UVA.

27. Lloyd C. Taylor, Jr., "Lila Hardaway Meade Valentine," in

James et al., *Notable American Women,* 3:504–505; Taylor, "Lila Meade Valentine: The FFV As Reformer," *VMHB* 70 (Oct. 1962): 473–479; Sarah McCulloh Lemmon, "Mary Cooke Branch Munford," in James et al., *Notable American Women,* 2:600–601; Bowie, *Sunrise in the South,* 64–76.

28. Belinda Bundy Friedman, "Orie Latham Hatcher and the Southern Woman's Educational Alliance" (Ph.D. diss., Duke University, 1981), 44.

29. Emily J. Salmon, ed., *A Hornbook of Virginia History,* 3d ed. (Richmond, 1983), 199–201.

30. Quoted in Bowie, *Sunrise in the South,* 116.

31. Ibid., 111–122; Anne Hobson Freeman, "Mary Munford's Fight for a College for Women Co-ordinate with the University of Virginia," *VMHB* 78 (Oct. 1970): 486 (quotation).

32. Wendell P. Dabney, *Maggie L. Walker and the I. O. of Saint Luke: The Woman and Her Work* (Cincinnati, 1927); Sadie Daniel St. Clair, "Maggie Lena Walker," in James et al., *Notable American Women,* 3:530–531.

33. *RTD,* 22 Oct. 1950, 17 June 1951.

34. Frances Watson, "Amanda Ellen Thorp: Richmond Motion Picture Pioneer," *Richmond Literature and History Quarterly* 1 (Fall 1978): 39–41.

35. Anne Goodwyn Jones, *Tomorrow is Another Day: The Woman Writer in the South, 1859–1936* (Baton Rouge, 1981), 235 (quotation); Annie Woodbridge, "Mary Johnston, A Universal Virginian," *Richmond Quarterly* 4 (Summer 1981): 23–33; Trudy J. Hanmer, "A Divine Discontent: Mary Johnston and Woman Suffrage in Virginia" (Master's thesis, University of Virginia, 1972).

36. The Glasgow literature is immense. Some starting points are Dorothy McInnis Scura, "The Southern Lady in the Early Novels of Ellen Glasgow," *Mississippi Quarterly* 31 (Winter 1977–1978): 17–31; Edgar E. MacDonald, "Ellen Glasgow's Spring Tonic: Blood and Irony," *Richmond Literature and History Quarterly* 1 (Summer 1978): 18–27; Marjorie R. Kaufman, "Ellen Anderson Gholson Glasgow," in James et al., *Notable American Women,* 2:44–49; Jones, *Tomorrow is Another Day,* 225–270; Linda W. Wagner, *Ellen Glasgow: Beyond Convention* (Austin, Tex., 1982); and Edgar E. MacDonald and Tonette Bond Inge, *Ellen Glasgow: A Reference Guide* (Boston, 1986).

37. Quoted in Scura, "The Southern Lady in the Early Novels of Ellen Glasgow," 17.

38. Carol Jean Clare, "The Woman Suffrage Movement in Virginia: Its Nature, Rationale, and Tactics" (Master's thesis, University of Virginia, 1968), 12–23.

39. Quoted in Hanmer, "A Divine Discontent," 29. *See also* Lucy Randolph Mason, *The Divine Discontent* (Richmond, n.d.), 16.

40. Lila M. Valentine to Roberta Wellford, 25 Apr. 1917, Roberta Wellford Papers, UVA; Margaret R. Johnson, "A Call to the Negro Women of Virginia," Mary-Cooke Branch Munford Papers, 1905–1930, Accession 28142, Personal Papers Collection, VSL.

41. *Fourth Annual Report of the Industrial Home School for Colored Girls*, 9.

42. Committee Reports, Woman's Committee, Council of National Defense, Virginia Division, Mary-Cooke Branch Munford Papers, VSL; Arthur Kyle Davis, ed., *Virginia Communities in War Time*, 1st ser. (Richmond, 1926); Jane Olcott, *The Work of Colored Women* (New York, 1919), 13–15, 36–39, 46–49, 52–54, 56–57.

43. Sykes, *Nancy: The Life of Lady Astor*, 181–207; Eleanor Flexner, *Century of Struggle: The Woman's Rights Movement in the United States* (New York, 1971), 314.

44. The posters are preserved in the Ida M. Thompson Collection of Virginia Woman Suffrage Papers, 1910–1925, Accession 22002, Personal Papers Collection, VSL. *See also* Lila Meade Valentine and Adèle Clark, "To Suffragists in Virginia," Roberta Wellford Papers, UVA; Clare, "The Woman Suffrage Movement in Virginia," 23–25; Anne Hamilton Stites, "The Inconceivable Revolution in Virginia, 1870–1920" (Master's thesis, University of Richmond, 1965), 146–152, 169.

45. Lemmon, "Mary Munford," 601; unidentified clipping, Kate Waller Barrett Papers, UVA; Sandra Gioia Treadway, "Sarah Lee Fain: Norfolk's First Woman Legislator," *VC* 30 (Winter 1981): 124–133.

46. Adèle Clark interview by Winston Broadfoot, 28 Feb. 1964, pp. 19–21, Southern Oral History Program Collection, UNC; Andrew Buni, *The Negro in Virginia Politics, 1902–1965* (Charlottesville, 1967), 73–81.

47. Adèle Clark interview by Winston Broadfoot, 24 (quotation), Southern Oral History Program Collection, UNC; Mary Elizabeth Pidgeon, "Virginia League of Women Voters," Aug. 1922, Mary Elizabeth Pidgeon Papers, Arthur and Elizabeth Schlesinger Library on the History of American Women, Radcliffe College, Cambridge, Mass.

48. "Calendar of Legislation—1925–26," Mary Elizabeth Pidgeon Papers.

49. Dabney, *Maggie L. Walker*, 136–137.

50. J. Lee Greene, "Anne Spencer of Lynchburg," *VC* 27 (Spring 1978): 178–185; Linda Peavy and Ursula Smith, *Women Who Changed Things* (New York, 1983), 61–78 [Orie Latham Hatcher]; Welford Dunaway Taylor, "Recalling Kate Langley Bosher," *Richmond Quarterly* 3 (Fall 1980): 33–38.

51. Anne Ruffin Sims, "Rosemont Workers," *Commonwealth* 4 (Feb. 1937): 12–13; *Smyth County News*, 3 Mar. 1983.

52. Mack Howard Sturgill, "Annabel Morris Buchanan and the White Top Festival" (unpublished paper, 1982), 2, 6 (quotations); David E. Whisnant, *All That Is Native & Fine: The Politics of Culture in an American Region* (Chapel Hill, 1983), 181–252.

53. *RTD*, 1 Jan. 1939, 26 July 1971; Lucy Randolph Mason, *To Win These Rights: A Personal Story of the CIO in the South* (New York, 1952), 22 (quotation). *See also* Nancy Ann White, "Lucy Randolph Mason," in Barbara Sicherman and Carol Hurd Green, eds. *Notable American Women: The Modern Period* (Cambridge, Mass., 1980), 461–462.

54. Charlotte Allen, comp., *A Record of Twenty-five Years: An Interpretation, Virginia Federation of Business and Professional Women, 1919–1944* (Richmond, 1946); *A History of the National Federation of Business and Professional Women's Clubs, Inc.* (New York, 1944).

55. Eudora Ramsay Richardson, "A Suffragist Takes A Challenge," *Commonwealth* 5 (May 1938): 24–26; Lois Scharf, *To Work and To Wed: Female Employment, Feminism, and the Great Depression* (Westport, Conn., 1980), 126; Ronald L. Heinemann, *Depression and New Deal in Virginia: The Enduring Dominion* (Charlottesville, 1983), 74–75, 91.

56. Allen, *A Record of Twenty-five Years*, 53.

57. T. M. Bost, Jr., "Salute to Our Foundrywomen!" *The Iron Worker* 6 (Summer 1943): 9.

58. "Curtain Rises on a New Scene; Enter: The Foundry Woman," *The Iron Worker* 6 (Spring 1943): 14.

59. The proportion of women architects declined from 3.5 percent to 3.1 percent; female clergy from 3.5 percent to 2.3 percent; and women lawyers from 4.5 percent to 2.8 percent. Calculated from the following publications of the United States Bureau of the Census:

Fourteenth Census of the United States Taken in the Year 1920, 4, Population, 1920, Occupations (Washington, D.C., 1921), 125; *Fifteenth Census of the United States: 1930, Population* (Washington, D.C., 1933), 4:1662; *Census of Population: 1950* (Washington, D.C., 1952), vol. 2, pt. 46, p. 229; *Census of Population: 1960* (Washington, D.C., 1963), vol. 1, pt. 48, p. 435.

60. Heinemann, *Depression and New Deal in Virginia*, 126–127; Susan Strasser, *Never Done: A History of American Housework* (New York, 1982).

61. Ruth Schwartz Cowan, "A Case Study of Technological and Social Change: The Washing Machine and the Working Wife," in Mary Hartman and Lois Banner, eds., *Clio's Consciousness Raised: New Perspectives on the History of Women* (New York, 1974), 245–253; Joann Vanek, "Time Spent in Housework," *Scientific American* 231 (Nov. 1974): 116–121.

62. Northington, *History of the Virginia Federation of Women's Clubs*, 152, 277, 281; Brownie Lee Jones interview by Mary Frederickson, 20 Apr. 1976, p. 48, Southern Oral History Program, UNC.

63. *Where We Stand: The Virginia Woman in the Seventies* (Charlottesville, 1977), 4, 7, 8.

64. Richmond Colored Teachers' Association, "Some Interesting Facts," Mary-Cooke Branch Munford Papers, VSL; Writers' Program of the Works Projects Administration in the State of Virginia, *The Negro in Virginia* (New York, 1940), 273–275.

65. Theresa Harris quoted in Louise Ellyson, "Women's Attitudes Range from Tolerance to Anger," *RTD*, 24 Nov. 1965.

66. Sarah Patton Boyle, *The Desegregated Heart: A Virginian's Stand in a Time of Transition* (New York, 1962); Virginius Dabney, *Virginia: The New Dominion* (Garden City, N.Y., 1971), 528–547; James Howard Hershman, Jr., "A Rumbling in the Museum: The Opponents of Virginia's Massive Resistance" (Ph.D. diss., University of Virginia, 1978).

67. A Look at the World's Week, *Life*, 7 Mar. 1960, 42–43; "Ruth Tinsley" (typescript), Richmond Chapter of Epicureans, Inc., Folder 315, Box 24, Accession 32425, Virginia Women's Cultural History Project, Inc., Papers, Organization Records, VSL.

68. Sara Evans, *Personal Politics: The Roots of Women's Liberation in the Civil Rights Movement and the New Left* (New York, 1979).

69. "Report of the Commission on the Status of Women to the

Governor and the General Assembly of Virginia" (House Document no. 20), in *House and Senate Documents, Virginia, Extra Session 1964, Extra Session 1965, Extra Session 1966* (Richmond, 1966), no. 20, p. 60; "First Report of the Virginia Commission on the Status of Women to the Governor, the General Assembly, and the Citizens of Virginia" (House Document no. 4), in *House and Senate Documents, Virginia, Regular Session 1971, Regular Session 1972*, 2 vols. (Richmond, 1971), vol. 2, no. 4, pp. 25, 35.

70. *Toward the Future: Final Report of the Virginia Women's Meeting, June 1977* (Arlington, Va., 1977).

71. Linda K. Kerber and Jane DeHart Mathews, eds., *Women's America: Refocusing the Past* (New York, 1982), contains the text of the 1973 decision, the ERA, and many other important legal documents.

72. Anne Dawson, "Efforts Against Sexual Assault by the Women of Virginia, 1970's–1980's," Virginians Aligned Against Sexual Assault, Arlington, Va., Folder 311, Box 24, Virginia Women's Cultural History Project, Inc., Papers, VSL.

73. For a list of female legislators from the files of the *Dictionary of Virginia Biography* project, I am grateful to Sandra Gioia Treadway, of the Virginia State Library.

Suggestions for Further Reading

GENERAL

Anderson, Della. *101 Virginia Women Writers: A Select Bibliography.* Richmond, 1984.

Banner, Lois W. *American Beauty.* New York, 1983.

Berman, Myron. *Richmond's Jewry, 1769–1976: Shabbat in Shockoe.* Charlottesville, 1979.

Cott, Nancy F., ed. *Root of Bitterness: Documents of the Social History of American Women.* New York, 1972.

James, Edward T., Janet Wilson James, and Paul S. Boyer, eds. *Notable American Women, 1607–1950: A Biographical Dictionary.* 3 vols. Cambridge, Mass., 1971.

Kerber, Linda K., and Jane DeHart Mathews, eds. *Women's America: Refocusing the Past.* New York, 1982.

Niederer, Frances J. *Hollins College: An Illustrated History.* Charlottesville, 1973.

Sicherman, Barbara, and Carol Hurd Green, eds. *Notable American Women: The Modern Period.* Cambridge, Mass., 1980.

Strasser, Susan. *Never Done: A History of American Housework.* New York, 1982.

NATIVE AMERICANS

Axtell, James, ed. *The Indian Peoples of Eastern America: A Documentary History of the Sexes.* New York, 1981.

Barbour, Philip L. *Pocahontas and Her World.* Boston, 1970.

Green, Rayna. "The Pocahontas Perplex: The Image of Indian Women in American Culture." *Massachusetts Review* 16 (Autumn 1975): 698–714.

Lurie, Nancy Oestreich. "Indian Cultural Adjustment to European Civilization." In *Seventeenth-Century America: Essays in Colonial History,* edited by James Morton Smith, 33–60. New York, 1959.

COLONIAL

Breen, T. H., and Stephen Innes. *"Myne Owne Ground": Race and Freedom on Virginia's Eastern Shore, 1640–1676.* New York, 1980.

Carr, Lois Green, and Lorena S. Walsh. "The Planter's Wife: The Experience of White Women in Seventeenth-Century Maryland." *William and Mary Quarterly,* 3d ser., 34 (Oct. 1977): 542–571.

Carson, Cary, and Lorena S. Walsh. "The Material Life of the Early American Housewife." *Winterthur Portfolio.* Forthcoming.

Dawe, Louise Belote, and Sandra Gioia Treadway. "Hannah Lee Corbin: The Forgotten Lee." *Virginia Cavalcade* 29 (Autumn 1979): 70–77.

Gundersen, Joan R. "The Non-Institutional Church: The Religious Role of Women in Eighteenth-Century Virginia." *Historical Magazine of the Protestant Episcopal Church* 51 (Dec. 1982): 347–357.

Kulikoff, Allan. "The Origins of Afro-American Society in Tidewater Maryland and Virginia, 1700–1790." *William and Mary Quarterly,* 3d ser., 35 (Apr. 1978): 226–259.

Morgan, Edmund S. *Virginians at Home: Family Life in the Eighteenth Century.* Williamsburg, 1952.

Rutman, Darrett B., and Anita H. Rutman. *A Place in Time: Middlesex County, Virginia, 1650–1750.* New York, 1984.

Smith, Daniel Blake. *Inside the Great House: Planter Family Life in Eighteenth-Century Chesapeake Society.* Ithaca, N.Y., 1980.

Speth, Linda E., and Alison Duncan Hirsch. *Women, Family, and Community in Colonial America: Two Perspectives.* New York, 1983.

Spruill, Julia Cherry. *Women's Life and Work in the Southern Colonies.* 1938. Reprint. New York, 1972.

Steele, Roberta Ingles, and Andrew Lewis Ingles, eds. *Escape from Indian Captivity: The Story of Mary Draper Ingles and Son Thomas Ingles As Told by John Ingles, Sr.* 2d ed. Radford, Va., 1982.

Walsh, Lorena S. " 'Till Death Us Do Part': Marriage and Family in Seventeenth-Century Maryland." In *The Chesapeake in the Seven-*

teenth Century: Essays on Anglo-American Society, edited by Thad W. Tate and David L. Ammerman, 126–152. New York, 1979.

Washburn, Wilcomb E. "The Humble Petition of Sarah Drummond." *William and Mary Quarterly,* 3d ser., 13 (July 1956): 354–375.

REVOLUTIONARY AND ANTEBELLUM AMERICA

Abraham, Mildred K. "The Library of Lady Jean Skipwith: A Book Collection from the Age of Jefferson." *Virginia Magazine of History and Biography* 91 (July 1983): 296–347.

Brown, Douglas Summers. "Elizabeth Henry Campbell Russell: Patroness of Early Methodism in the Highlands of Virginia." *Virginia Cavalcade* 30 (Winter 1981): 110–117.

Clinton, Catherine. *The Plantation Mistress: Woman's World in the Old South.* New York, 1982.

Cometti, Elizabeth. *Social Life in Virginia During the War for Independence.* Williamsburg, 1978.

Foner, Philip S., and Josephine F. Pacheco. *Three Who Dared: Prudence Crandall, Margaret Douglass, Myrtilla Miner—Champions of Antebellum Black Education.* Westport, Conn., 1984.

Friedman, Jean E. *The Enclosed Garden: Women and Community in the Evangelical South, 1830–1900.* Chapel Hill, 1985.

Genovese, Eugene D. *Roll, Jordan, Roll: The World the Slaves Made.* New York, 1974.

Hunt-Jones, Conover. *Dolley and the Great Little Madison.* Washington, D.C., 1977.

Husted, Margaret. "Mary Randolph's *The Virginia Housewife:* America's First Regional Cookbook." *Virginia Cavalcade* 30 (Autumn 1980): 76–87.

Jones, Jacqueline. *Labor of Love, Labor of Sorrow: Black Women, Work, and the Family from Slavery to the Present.* New York, 1985.

Kerber, Linda K. *Women of the Republic: Intellect and Ideology in Revolutionary America.* Chapel Hill, 1980.

Lebsock, Suzanne. *The Free Women of Petersburg: Status and Culture in a Southern Town, 1784–1860.* New York, 1984.

Lewis, Jan. *The Pursuit of Happiness: Family and Values in Jefferson's Virginia.* Cambridge, Eng., and New York, 1983.

McGraw, Marie Tyler. "Northern Virginia Colonizationists." *Northern Virginia Heritage* 5 (Feb. 1983): 9–10, 16–18.

Norton, Mary Beth. *Liberty's Daughters: The Revolutionary Experience of American Women, 1750–1800.* Boston, 1980.

Perdue, Charles L., Jr., Thomas E. Barden, and Robert K. Phillips, eds. *Weevils in the Wheat: Interviews with Virginia Ex-Slaves.* Bloomington, Ind., 1980.

Pusey, William W. *Elusive Aspirations: The History of the Female Academy in Lexington, Virginia.* Lexington, Va., 1983.

Rachal, William M. E. "Virginia's First College for Women: The Female Collegiate Institute in Buckingham County." *Virginia Cavalcade* 2 (Summer 1952): 44–47.

Scott, Anne Firor. *The Southern Lady: From Pedestal to Politics, 1830–1930.* Chicago, 1970.

Welter, Barbara. "The Cult of True Womanhood: 1820–1860." *American Quarterly* 18 (Summer 1966): 151–174.

White, Deborah G. *Ar'n't I a Woman? Female Slaves in the Plantation South.* New York, 1985.

Civil War and Reconstruction

Bailey, James H. "Crazy Bet, Union Spy." [Elizabeth Van Lew]. *Virginia Cavalcade* 1 (Spring 1952): 14–17.

Chesson, Michael B. "Harlots or Heroines? A New Look at the Richmond Bread Riot." *Virginia Magazine of History and Biography* 92 (Apr. 1984): 131–175.

Coleman, Elizabeth Dabney. "The Captain Was a Lady." *Virginia Cavalcade* 6 (Summer 1956): 35–41.

Engs, Robert Francis. *Freedom's First Generation: Black Hampton, Virginia, 1861–1890.* Philadelphia, 1979.

Massey, Mary Elizabeth. *Bonnet Brigades.* New York, 1966.

Pember, Phoebe Yates. *A Southern Woman's Story: Life in Confederate Richmond.* Jackson, Tenn., 1959.

Robertson, Mary D., ed. *Lucy Breckinridge of Grove Hill: The Journal of a Virginia Girl, 1862–1864.* Kent, Ohio, 1979.

Scarborough, Ruth. *Belle Boyd: Siren of the South.* Macon, Ga., 1983.

Scura, Dorothy McInnis. "Constance Cary Harrison: A Spirited Lady of Letters." *Richmond Literature and History Quarterly* 1 (Winter 1978): 16–20.

Wiley, Bell Irvin. *The Plain People of the Confederacy.* Baton Rouge, 1943.

Woodward, C. Vann, ed. *Mary Chesnut's Civil War.* New Haven, 1981.

THE LATE NINETEENTH CENTURY

Barrett, Janie Porter. *Locust Street Social Settlement, Hampton, Virginia.* Hampton, Va., 1912.

Bratton, Mary Jo Jackson. " 'Marion Harland': A Literary Woman of the Old Dominion." *Virginia Cavalcade* 35 (Winter 1986): 136–143.

Dabney, Wendell P. *Maggie L. Walker and the I. O. of Saint Luke: The Woman and Her Work.* Cincinnati, 1927.

Jervey, Edward D. "Elmina Slenker: Freethinker and Sex Radical." *Virginia Social Science Journal* 16 (Apr. 1981): 1–12.

Jones, Anne Goodwyn. *Tomorrow is Another Day: The Woman Writer in the South, 1859–1936.* Baton Route, 1981.

Kimbrough, Janet C. "The Early History of the Association for the Preservation of Virginia Antiquities: A Personal Account." *Virginia Cavalcade* 30 (Autumn 1980): 68–75.

Langhorne, Orra. *Southern Sketches from Virginia, 1881–1901.* Edited by Charles E. Wynes. Charlottesville, 1964.

Longest, George C. *Three Virginia Writers; Mary Johnston, Thomas Nelson Page, and Amélie Rives Troubetzkoy: A Reference Guide.* Boston, 1978.

Morse, Nita Ligon, and Eda Carter Williams. *The History of Sheltering Arms Hospital: The First 75 Years, 1889–1964.* N.p., n.d.

"Rosa D. Bowser: Talent to Spare, Talent to Share." *Richmond Literature and History Quarterly* 1 (Fall 1978): 45–46.

Taylor, Welford Dunaway. *Amélie Rives (Princess Troubetzkoy).* New York, 1973.

Williams, Etta Rebecca. "Fannie Criss: Turn of the Century Dressmaker." *Richmond Quarterly* 4 (Spring 1982): 46–48.

Wilson, Otto. *Life of Dr. Kate Waller Barrett.* New York, 1974.

Wright, R. Lewis. "A Portfolio from the Virginia Sketchbook of Edith Clark Chadwick." *Virginia Cavalcade* 29 (Spring 1980): 150–155.

THE TWENTIETH CENTURY

Bowie, Walter Russell. *Sunrise in the South: The Life of Mary-Cooke Branch Munford.* Richmond, 1942.

Boyle, Sarah Patton. *The Desegregated Heart: A Virginian's Stand in a Time of Transition.* New York, 1962.

"First Report of the Virginia Commission on the Status of Women to the Governor, the General Assembly, and the Citizens of Virginia" (House Document no. 4). In *House and Senate Documents, Vir-*

ginia, *Regular Session 1971, Regular Session 1972.* 2 vols. Richmond, 1971.

Flexner, Eleanor. *Century of Struggle: The Woman's Rights Movement in the United States.* New York, 1971.

Freeman, Anne Hobson. "Mary Munford's Fight for a College for Women Co-ordinate with the University of Virginia." *Virginia Magazine of History and Biography* 78 (Oct. 1970): 481–491.

Greene, J. Lee. "Anne Spencer of Lynchburg." *Virginia Cavalcade* 27 (Spring 1978): 178–185.

———. *Time's Unfading Garden: Anne Spencer's Life and Poetry.* Baton Rouge, 1977.

Jones, Lance G. E. *The Jeanes Teacher in the United States, 1908–1933: An Account of Twenty-five Years' Experience in the Supervision of Negro Rural Schools.* Chapel Hill, 1937.

Langhorne, Elizabeth. "Nancy Langhorne Astor: A Virginian in England." *Virginia Cavalcade* 23 (Winter 1974): 38–47.

Lyle, Royster, Jr. "Of Manor Houses and Gardens: Edith Sale, Pioneer in the Study of Virginia Mansions." *Virginia Cavalcade* 34 (Winter 1985): 126–135.

MacDonald, Edgar E., and Tonette Bond Inge. *Ellen Glasgow: A Reference Guide.* Boston, 1986.

Mason, Lucy Randolph. *To Win These Rights: A Personal Story of the CIO in the South.* New York, 1952.

Morton, Rosalie Slaughter. *A Woman Surgeon: The Life and Work of Rosalie Slaughter Morton.* New York, 1937.

Northington, Etta Belle Walker. *A History of the Virginia Federation of Women's Clubs, 1907–1957.* Richmond, 1958.

Ribblett, David L. "From Cross Creek to Richmond: Marjorie Kinnan Rawlings Researches Ellen Glasgow." *Virginia Cavalcade* 36 (Summer 1986): 4–15.

Rosenberg, Rosalind. *Beyond Separate Spheres: Intellectual Roots of Modern Feminism.* New Haven, 1982.

Ryburn, Mrs. White M. [Jessie D.], Ellen S. Bowen, and Mrs. J. W. Walker. *Women of Old Abingdon.* Pulaski, Va., 1937.

Scharf, Lois. *To Work and To Wed: Female Employment, Feminism, and the Great Depression.* Westport, Conn., 1980.

Scott, Anne Firor, and Andrew MacKay Scott. *One Half the People: The Fight for Woman Suffrage.* Urbana, Ill., 1983.

Scura, Dorothy McInnis. "The Southern Lady in the Early Novels of

Ellen Glasgow." *Mississippi Quarterly* 31 (Winter 1977–1978): 17–32.

Sims, Anne Ruffin. "Rosemont Workers." *Commonwealth* 4 (Feb. 1937): 12–13.

Sykes, Christopher. *Nancy: The Life of Lady Astor.* London and New York, 1972.

Taylor, Lloyd C., Jr. "Lila Meade Valentine: The FFV As Reformer." *Virginia Magazine of History and Biography* 70 (Oct. 1962): 471–487.

Toward the Future: Final Report of the Virginia Women's Meeting, June 1977. Arlington, Va., 1977.

Treadway, Sandra Gioia. "Sarah Lee Fain: Norfolk's First Woman Legislator." *Virginia Cavalcade* 30 (Winter 1981): 124–133.

Index

Virginia Women, 1600–1945: "A Share of Honour"
was set in Garamond by Coghill Composition Company, Richmond.
Bob Sheppard, of Richmond, designed the covers.
Patricia V. Higgs, of Williamsburg, prepared the index.
Typesetting and indexing costs were partially defrayed by a grant from the
Virginia Foundation for Humanities and Public Policy, Charlottesville.
The book was printed and bound by
John D. Lucas Printing Company, Baltimore,
on fifty-pound Warren Olde Style text,
with illustrations on seventy-pound Warren Flokote,
and covers of sixty-five-pound laid-finish Neenah Classic Cover.